T0328653

Cambridge Elements ≡

Elements in Theatre, Performance and the Political
edited by
Trish Reid
University of Reading
Liz Tomlin
University of Glasgow

UTPAL DUTT AND POLITICAL THEATRE IN POSTCOLONIAL INDIA

Mallarika Sinha Roy
Jawaharlal Nehru University

CAMBRIDGE
UNIVERSITY PRESS

Shaftesbury Road, Cambridge CB2 8EA, United Kingdom

One Liberty Plaza, 20th Floor, New York, NY 10006, USA

477 Williamstown Road, Port Melbourne, VIC 3207, Australia

314–321, 3rd Floor, Plot 3, Splendor Forum, Jasola District Centre, New Delhi – 110025, India

103 Penang Road, #05–06/07, Visioncrest Commercial, Singapore 238467

Cambridge University Press is part of Cambridge University Press & Assessment, a department of the University of Cambridge.

We share the University's mission to contribute to society through the pursuit of education, learning and research at the highest international levels of excellence.

www.cambridge.org
Information on this title: www.cambridge.org/9781009500227

DOI: 10.1017/9781009264068

When citing this work, please include a reference to the DOI 10.1017/9781009264068

First published 2024

A catalogue record for this publication is available from the British Library.

ISBN 978-1-009-50022-7 Hardback
ISBN 978-1-009-26407-5 Paperback
ISSN 2753-1244 (online)
ISSN 2753-1236 (print)

Cambridge University Press & Assessment has no responsibility for the persistence or accuracy of URLs for external or third-party internet websites referred to in this publication and does not guarantee that any content on such websites is, or will remain, accurate or appropriate.

Utpal Dutt and Political Theatre in Postcolonial India

Elements in Theatre, Performance and the Political

DOI: 10.1017/9781009264068
First published online: March 2024

Mallarika Sinha Roy
Jawaharlal Nehru University

Author for correspondence: Mallarika Sinha Roy, msroy@jnu.ac.in

Abstract: Among the most significant playwrights and theatre-makers of postcolonial India, Utpal Dutt (1929–1993) was an early exponent of rethinking colonial history through political theatre. Dutt envisaged political theatre as part of the larger Marxist project, and his incorporation of new developments in Marxist thinking, including the contributions of Antonio Gramsci, makes it possible to conceptualize his protagonists as insurgent subalterns. A decolonial approach to staging history remained a significant element in Dutt's artistic project. This Element examines Dutt's passionate engagement with Marxism and explores how this sense of urgency was actioned through the writing and producing of plays about the peasant revolts and armed anti-colonial movements which took place during the period of British rule. Drawing on contemporary debates in political theatre regarding the autonomy of the spectator and the performance of history, the author locates Dutt's political theatre in a historical frame.

Keywords: political theatre, postcolonial India, decolonization, Utpal Dutt, Indian theatre

ISBNs: 9781009500227 (HB), 9781009264075 (PB), 9781009264068 (OC)
ISSNs: 2753-1244 (online), 2753-1236 (print)

Contents

Introduction

Why Utpal Dutt? Why Now?

On 17 January 2023, Theatre Formation Paribartak, a West Bengal based group, staged *Titu Mir* (1978) (See Figure 1), at Academy of Fine Arts in Kolkata. The play, written by Utpal Dutt (1929–1993) (See Figure 2), is about Islamic religious reformer Mir Nisar Ali, also known as Titu Mir, who organized and led a peasant revolt against the British East India Company in the Barasat region of Bengal from 1827 to 1831. It challenges existing conservative historical accounts, dependent on colonial archives, that portray Titu Mir as an anti-Hindu zealot, and focuses instead on his subaltern vision of anti-colonial struggle where the rural dispossessed of all religions could come together.

About an hour into the play, as the contradictions between colonial forces – both militarized and cultural – and Titu Mir's guerrilla band of peasant rebels intensify, a critical moment arrives with the possibility of a monumental historical moment of struggle. The stage space is dominated by a huge bamboo structure. A horizontally slanted bamboo rostrum divides the stage space between an interior and exterior. Titu Mir doubles his long robe, baring his legs from the knee to give a sartorial-symbolic gesture of militancy, and ties it to his waist and walks up the rostrum. Roaring with the desire for vengeance, Titu Mir sways his bamboo staff, and finally leaps out to the front of the stage. The lights concentrate on his leaping figure, making him larger than life.

As the curtain closes for the interval, the full house applauds in unison. It is a spontaneous response which might seem to indicate that the twenty-first-century Bengali audience has found a mimetic connection with a two-hundred-year-old peasant rebel; but because the scene emphasizes the inevitable death of Titu Mir, the unmaking of this connection is built into the staging of the heightened moment. The audience knows that the end will come in the form of defeat, but the presentation of a historical moment unfolding right in front of them creates a connection which is both informed and exhilarating. This is a classic example of Utpal Dutt's dramaturgy – political theatre that never allows its audience to immerse in reliving a moment of the past, but rather, continuously compels reflection on its significance for the present.

Let us remind ourselves that the play was written in 1978 and Dutt died in 1993. The full house indicates a triumphant return of Dutt's work on Bengali stage with a new relevance in the second decade of twenty-first century as the right-wing government of India had returned to power for the second consecutive term with an increased majority, and Hindutva become pervasive in nearly every aspect of Indian public life. The relevance lies in exploration of people's collective emotions to combat the fascist propaganda in contemporary India

Figure 1 Titumir, 2019, Theatre Formation Paribartak

Figure 2 Utpal Dutt

(Bhattacharjee 2019). The return to his work is, in fact, not limited to *Titu Mir*. Several other of his plays are running in Kolkata in 2023.

Utpal Dutt's engagement with political theatre, his reliance on history to comment on the contemporary and his craft as a theatre-maker provide us with a timely and important opportunity to reflect on a postcolonial cultural politics that invested in the process of decolonization. Dutt's political theatre is well placed to avail this opportunity because his output – from 1959 to 1989 – coincides with a period of energetic negotiating with and challenging the legacies of colonial modernity. Drawing from Partha Chatterjee's discussion of 'Our Modernity' (1997), I would like to argue that colonial modernity refers to the ways in which the British colonial rule had its impact on deciding the shifts and changes in the social, economic and cultural life in India. The introduction of English education has been quite central in defining the features of the cultural life where theatre as a form of public entertainment as well as a mode of disseminating messages of history became a primary site of practicing modernity. The biography of modern Indian theatre in the post-independence period is replete with debates on defining tradition and modernity, on identifying contact points between politics and culture, and on extrapolating the nature of engagements with nationalism and socialism. This Element seeks to show that contextualizing Utpal Dutt within this historical canvas can open up distinctive ways of thinking through political theatre in a postcolonial condition.

The Voice of Decolonization: Utpal Dutt in Post-independence Modern Indian Theatre

Modern Indian theatre, as we have come to know it, bears a colonial legacy and there is plenty of scholarly work on the specific trajectories through which the legacy manifested itself in representational conventions, stagecraft, acting styles and the imagination of theatricality (Bhatia 2004; Dharwadker 2005; Chatterjee 2016). Keeping in mind the multiplicity of languages, locations, traditions of performance and cultures of orality in Indian theatre, it is equally important to remember that in the post-independence period (after 1947) the idea of the modern in Indian theatre relentlessly interacted with, negotiated with and at times, struggled against, the tradition of pre-colonial 'folk theatre' on the one hand, and the tradition of classical Sanskrit drama going back to two millennia on the other. Indian playwrights and theatre-makers have engaged intensely with the various forms and styles of the 'folk theatre' and re-articulated the classical tradition to create a framework that might support the notion of the national modern as an assertion of the simultaneous coexistence of multiple modernities. This idea of multiple modernities imagines different outcomes for different histories in different spatio-temporal contexts and allows us to conceptualize the modern beyond colonial modernity, and also to think of decolonization as a process, not limited by the singular event of achieving national independence at a specific time.

The inspiration for decolonization, as a philosophical term, writes Achille Mbembe, was the 'active will to community' which can be translated as something like 'to stand up on one's own and create a heritage' (2021: 2–3). The impetus for decolonization in theatre, as it moved from re-instituting indigenous traditions in place of colonial modernity, to retrieving indigenous systems through 'provincializing Europe' as Dipesh Chakrabarty aptly defines

(2002), came from different quarters. The Cold War context provided a range of influences, from western European and north American theatre experiments to socialist realisms and socialist internationalism, as well as the intercultural practices emerging from Asian–African alliances. The modern Indian theatre drew on these multiple modernities. The outcome was a significant shift away not only from traditional forms of folk theatre and classical Sanskrit drama, but also from the modern colonial theatre in terms of canon formation, actor training, circulation of texts and performances, reception, patronage and criticism. Institutionally, as part of the 'will to community', a new cultural bureaucracy, often functioning closely with the administrative one, sustained this shift from the local to the national level. This cultural bureaucracy involved setting up of national bodies like the Sangeet Natak Academy in 1953, which took up the responsibilities of preserving and promoting the cultural heritage of dance, music and performing arts.

Utpal Dutt (1929–1993) embodied this shift. With the exception of direct involvement in cultural bureaucracy, he straddled the process of decolonization, forging a political theatre of the postcolonial contemporary for modern India. When he emerged as a promising theatre-maker and performer in the city of Calcutta in late 1940s, the Indian People's Theatre Association (IPTA henceforth), as part of the communist movement in India, had already established itself as a formidable force in cultural politics and the idea of progressive political theatre had started to gain ground. Before his inevitable shift towards IPTA in 1950–1951, Dutt was a member of British thespian Geoffrey Kendal's touring Shakespeareana International, which performed Shakespeare's plays in metropolises and *mofussil* towns across India. Theatre critic Samik Bandyopadhyay notes that the democratic nature of this travelling theatre troupe was crucial in shaping Dutt as an artist (2017). After touring with Kendal, Dutt started his own English theatre group in Calcutta, The Amateur Shakespeareans, and won critical acclaim for modernized productions of *Romeo and Juliet* (1948) and *Julius Caesar* (1949).

Let me pause briefly and focus on the 1949 *Julius Caesar* production. Dutt had begun to read about the Russian Revolution in school and graduating to college had also meant graduating to reading the political philosophy of Marx. The result of this political engagement was evident in the production of *Julius Caesar* which was costumed in twentieth-century Italian Fascist uniforms. Caesar wore with a felt hat and his senators, clad in red and black, greeted him with the raised one-arm salute. The Forum speeches of Mark Antony and Brutus were represented as radio broadcasts, and the scenography of the battle scene in Philippi referred to a war-damaged town with the sound effects of bombing and machine-gun fire (2005: 443–444). Without changing a word of

Shakespeare's text, the production made the history of dictatorship and democratic struggle against totalitarianism relevant for theatre of a post-colony, still reeling under the aftermath of the Partition. It staged apprehension about the rise of demagogues at a critical moment at the beginning of Indian democracy. The processes of decolonization had found a powerful voice.

Dutt's acute sense of the need to engage with the process of decolonization was also the reason behind his abandonment of English theatre even after such bravura productions. English theatre in Calcutta was a decidedly elite practice and he turned away from it to begin his stint with IPTA, joining the central Calcutta squad of IPTA as a director and actor and performing in different productions like Tagore's *Bisarjan* (performed in 1952) and Ritwik Ghatak's *Dalil* (1951) as well as in various street-corner plays like *Bhoter Bhet* (1951). This period was an exhilarating one for Dutt as he writes in *Towards a Revolutionary Theatre* that he met:

> Panu Pal, the creator of street-corner plays; Ritwik Ghatak, lanky awkward, fiercely puritanical and therefore critical of my decadent habits, thinking cinematically all the time; Mrinal Sen, wizard with shadow-plays, forerunners of his wonderful films … Hemango Biswas, discovering fantastic melodies from the depths of the countryside; Nirmal Ghosh, organizing, cajoling, threatening, even lying and tricking to keep the great organization going. (2009: 39)

He also met Niranjan Sen, who headed the organization. However, his youthful enthusiasm for ideological debates on Marxism was not received well in IPTA, 'When the twenty-one-year-old Dutt marched into the Party office on 46 Dharamtala Street with a copy of Trotsky's *Permanent Revolution* in his hand', Rustom Bharucha observes, 'he was asking for trouble' (1983: 58). He was branded a Trotskyite, which Dutt maintained was quite untrue, and accused of smoking and drinking, which he confessed was quite true. He was expelled from IPTA after about eight months.

The experience of making theatre with IPTA while engaging with communist politics and Marxist philosophy, though short-lived, became foundational in Dutt's subsequent journey as a political theatre artist. He created his 'Little Theatre Group' (LTG) and, in 1953 leased the Minerva theatre in Calcutta as its permanent home. LTG began with classic Tagore plays, translations of Shakespeare and Russian theatre, and social farces by the nineteenth-century playwright Michael Madhusudan Dutt. Their production of *Macbeth* (1954) became particularly successful and received invitations for performances even in remote villages, smaller towns and working-class areas (Sen 2017: 39). LTG finally found its feet on the Bengali stage with Dutt's *Angaar* (1959), a play about the lives of coal miners that culminates in a mining disaster and references a recent catastrophe in the Baradhemo coal mine. *Angaar* became hugely popular not only for its intensely political theme but also because of the sophisticated scenography, sound and lighting design employed. The climax of *Angaar*, an exemplary feat of stagecraft depicting the despair of seven miners trapped underground waiting to be drowned, is described by Bharucha as an 'epiphany of grief' in which the spectacle of a calamity becomes a source of entertainment and is applauded (1983: 68). Dutt, in his later assessment of his own work, was critical of *Angaar* because it could not represent the truth of miners' resistance, but was limited to displaying the facts of their huge exploitation.

This tension between truth and fact shaped Dutt's vision of political theatre, which he called revolutionary theatre. He differentiated between fact and truth by focusing on their connection with social conflict and argued that fact remains mere bourgeois truth when abstracted from the context of continuous social conflict between the haves and the have-nots and conversely that fact can become a revolutionary truth when it intertwines the realities of conflict, and sides unerringly with the have-nots (2009: 60–67). His aim was to represent revolutionary truth because, in his view, presenting only impartial facts risked reifying bourgeois power, and he wanted his theatre to be an agent of change, and thus a factor in the revolution. This meant recounting as many instances of such change as possible, especially historical moments when exploitative regimes are challenged by the poor, the colonized and the 'native'. He aspired to portray the full complexity of power relations at intersecting points in the context of social conflict. This is the reason Dutt so often revisits histories of anti-colonial revolts against the British in India, revolts against other imperial powers in other geopolitical contexts and rebellions against experiences of domination. His stint in the Bengali folk theatre form Jatra, from 1971 to 1988, bears the same marks of revolutionary intent in highlighting historical moments of resistance against colonial/authoritarian regimes.

Dutt's description of Jatra as a form suited to 'immediately reflecting the social conflict of its time in vigorous, violent terms' indicates his interest in the political efficacy of popular folk theatre (2009: 170). He became directly involved in the early 1970s when he started writing play-texts for different Jatra companies and directing them. His growing familiarity with the form resulted in a deeper understanding of its potential for shaping any content according to its own conventions and presenting its huge urban and rural working-class audience with new interpretations of social conflict within an intelligible grammar of actions. Beginning with *Rifle* (1968), which focused on the anti-colonial armed revolutionary movement in the 1930s, and *Delhi Chalo*

(1971), about the anti-colonial war of Indian National Army (INA) led by Subhash Chandra Bose, Dutt went on to write several *Jatra* plays including *Bhuli Nai Priya* (1970), *Jallianwallahbag* (1969), *Sannyasir Tarabari* (1972) and *Mukti Diksha* (1974). *Bhuli Nai Priya* is an adaptation of *Romeo and Juliet*, *Jallianwallahbag* deals with the killing of hundreds of unarmed Indian nationalists by the police in Jallianwallahbag, Punjab, in 1919, *Sannyasir Tarabari* tells of the Sannyasi-Fakir rebellion against the British East India Company in late eighteenth-century Bengal, and *Mukti Diksha* of French revolutionaries in the Paris Commune of 1871.

It may be useful, at this point in the discussion, to consider certain critical reflections on the nature of post-independence modern Indian theatre to situate Dutt's engagement with history, especially colonial history (Bharucha 1983, 1993; Bhatia 1999; Dharwadker 2005). Rustom Bharucha, from his early writings on Bengali political theatre (1983) to his critique of simplistic interculturalism (1993), has repeatedly focused on the specificity of history – language, location, tradition as well as everyday struggles of the people of a particular location – in any form of writing about Indian theatre, more specifically post-independence Indian theatre. His commentary on Dutt is, thus, scrupulously contextualized through the ideological and political legacies that influenced Bengali theatre from the colonial period. Bhatia, in her long essay on Dutt's history play *Mahavidroha* (The Great Rebellion, 1973), meticulously tracks Dutt's challenge to the 'Western' or colonial interpretation of the rebellion of 1857 through narrative strategy and character formation (1999). For Dharwadker, however, Indian theatre-makers have both embraced and rejected the colonial legacy 'in terms of form, language, ideology and conventions of representation' (2005: 11). Rather than focusing solely on anti-colonial critique or experiences of exploitation, she argues, post-independence Indian theatre has made efforts to engage with the full spectrum of India–West encounter. This broader perspective is evidenced by the fact 'the vast majority of contemporary plays are not concerned with colonialism at all but with the intersecting structures of home, family, and nation in the urban society of the present or with the configurations of gender and desire in the reimagined "folk" cultures of an unspecified past' (2005: 11). Dharwadker references a wide range of playwrights, including Mohan Rakesh, Badal Sircar, Vijay Tendulkar, Girish Karnad, Habib Tanvir, G. P. Deshpande and Mahesh Elkunchwar as well as directors like Shombhu Mitra, Ebrahim Alkazi, K. N. Panikkar, B. V. Karanth, Vijaya Mehta, Satyadev Dube, Usha Ganguli and Neelam Mansingh Chowdhry and Dutt, himself. She also observes that the use of two narrative forms – myth and history – constitutes the major thematics of postcolonial modern Indian theatre.

I will refer to Bharucha's work on Dutt extensively in the following sections and also reflect on Bhatia's reading of Dutt's imagining of history. It will suffice, consequently, to mention here that in response to Dharwadker's characterization of post-independence modern Indian theatre, I would like to point out that the colonial legacies are very much part of the post-independence modern Indian theatre even when the 'majority' of practitioners were not explicitly engaging with them in the first three decades after independence. If the contemporary urban family, nation, home and the re-imagined 'folk' are indeed the major themes of modern Indian theatre, then it must engage with colonialism because decolonization as a process involves all these sites. Myth, in such a context, is not an 'unspecified time' and 'folk' not a timeless continuity. The constructive elements of myth are historical and folk as an idea as well as a set of practices has a material history and demands rigorous historiography. Situating them in the postcolonial contemporary inevitably involves 'grasping the political present' paying 'close attention to historical continuities, repetitions, and reactivations' (Wilder and Watson 2018: 1). Utpal Dutt's sustained engagement with history, as a complex network of relations of power and anti-colonial/ anti-imperialist resistance, and his reflections on working with myths in revolutionary theatre firmly locate him in the pantheon of postcolonial Indian theatre-makers but his vision of revolutionary political theatre also distinguishes him. My effort in this Element is directed towards exploring this particular distinguishing feature of Dutt's practice.

Exploring a Self-confessed 'Propagandist': Revolutionary Theatre of Utpal Dutt

As Dutt stepped into the Minerva Theatre (built in 1893 at Beadon street, which was the veritable theatre district of nineteenth and early twentieth-century Calcutta) with his LTG, he also entered into conversation with the history of Bengali theatre from the nineteenth century, reinventing it and giving it new direction. The popular success of *Angaar* gave him scope for developing elaborate stagecraft and collaborating with leading figures from different fields to develop a specific understanding of theatre beyond spectacle but not without it. These included the sitar maestro Ravi Shankar (1930–2012) who composed music for *Angaar*, the lighting designer Tapas Sen (1924–2006) and the scenographer Nirmal Guha Roy. He later worked with the renowned folk singer Nirmalendu Choudhury (1922–1981) on the production of *Titas Ekti Nadir Nam* (1963) and the singer, composer and political activist Hemanga Biswas (1912–1987) on *Kallol* (1965) and *Teer* (1967). Dutt's dramaturgy found greater and more acute expression as his political consciousness began to significantly inform his work.

'One of the ironies of political theatre', observes Rustom Bharucha, 'is that it thrives during the worst periods of repression' (1983: 73). Discussions of political theatre, consequently, need to be continually informed by understanding of the nature of repression and period-specific details of each sociopolitical situation. In order to make sense of the cultural critique offered by political theatre, the critic has to engage with the defining characteristics of the postcolonial contemporary. This need becomes even more acute in the case of an artist like Dutt because he explicitly identified his project as a revolutionary theatre, which 'addresses these working masses and must adjust its pitch, tone and volume accordingly' in order to agitate for revolutionary social transformation (2009: 82). That his revolutionary theatre was dismissed by a large number of critics as communist propaganda did not dishearten Dutt, but rather he wore the term 'propagandist' as a badge of honour and declared 'to hell with the so-called critics who find our plays naive, melodramatic and loud' (2009: 82).

LTG broke up during the politically tumultuous period of 1969–1970 when the Naxalbari movement created intense ideological debate within communism and resulted in indiscriminate political violence, followed by brutal state repression. Dutt's initial fascination with Naxalite ideology and practice soon turned into disillusionment and he formed the new group People's Little Theatre (PLT) in 1971. The political focus of his theatre continued well into the late 1980s, when socialism across the world faced its worst crisis with the demise of Soviet Union and the disintegration of the Eastern Block in Europe.

My method of exploring Dutt's revolutionary political theatre in this Element depends on thinking beyond the binaries that define older debates between the universal and particular in terms of neutral theatre and propaganda plays, between Marxism and Postcolonial Theory in terms of universalist theories of liberation based on European Enlightenment principles and the particularistic historical critiques of Western modernity in the Global South, and between politics and cultures in terms of exclusive separate spheres of performance and knowledge production. Instead, let us consider these binaries as complementary dyads that enable thinking about revolutionary theatre as a significant part of the process of decolonization. Dutt's intellectual world supports this approach because he continually engages with Shakespearean classics, Brechtian political theatre and Russian and East-European socialist theatre, but always relies on Indian social realities, as they have unfolded historically, to produce his own theatre. In his own way, he interprets the revolutionary truth in historical moments of resistance as not only what had factually happened but also what *might* have happened and thus creates a bridge between universalist abstractions and particularly located historical experiences.

The geopolitical events that circumscribe particular sociopolitical moments in specific contexts become useful in unpacking the way revolutionary theatre responded to events and what they implied for the Indian people, namely the audience of Dutt's revolutionary theatre. Dutt's theatre operated against the backdrop of Cold War cultural rivalries, and his imagination of revolution was firmly located in socialist internationalism. In the recent years, Cold War studies has shifted focus from the power struggle between the USA and USSR to explore the ways the Cold War affected decolonization in newly independent nation states in Asia, Africa and the Americas, and the now forgotten alignments of the Global South with East Europe and Soviet Russia through cultural exchanges. 'The Cold War's specific character of state militarism, competitive nationalisms, socialist utopianism and vehement anticommunism', argues Watson and Wilder, 'dramatically shaped alignments and forged new moral and political boundaries' that generated responses in the postcolonial revolutionary theatre (2018: 21–22).

Geopolitics also shaped Dutt's thinking on the reciprocal relationship between theatre and its audience. Dutt envisaged a dynamic relationship with the audience. In *Towards a Revolutionary Theatre* (2009), he gave several instances how characterizations of international figures in his theatre relied on audience experience and memories of more local and familiar similar figures. How an American lawyer would be portrayed on stage, the behaviour of an American general posted in Vietnam, the internal dynamics of a German communist group, the response of a British colonial Captain to an Agent of British East India Company, would all depend on the ways the audience could connect them with figures from their known world. This dynamic relationship can be accessed methodologically only when the worlds of politics and culture are viewed as aligned spheres with myriad contact points.

Placing Dutt's theatre at these contact zones between history, imagination and politics in postcolonial India also involves outlining my approach to his works in this Element. It is crucial, for instance, to remember that these contact zones emerge through interconnected histories of modern European empires. Along with multiple modernities, thus, the nebulous thread of interconnections weave in Shakespeare with Brecht with socialist Russian and German theatre as well as post-imperial British theatre. Dutt's drawing from multiple ideological and aesthetic strands of modern theatre, most specifically in his revolutionary theatre, needs to be understood in the context of both the location and mobility of Dutt as a postcolonial intellectual (See Figure 3). His insistence on having 'people' in the title of the theatre group he reconstituted in 1971 evidences the ways in which he had thus far imagined people as the principal protagonist of his theatre-making project. This imagination reminds us how communities or collectives consolidate at intersecting points between class, race, caste, ethnicity, gender, region, religion,

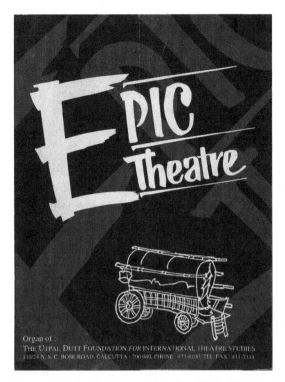

Figure 3 Epic Theatre, a journal published by Dutt

nation and imperial histories, and while it is necessary to locate them it is also important to imagine the people beyond such scales and boundaries. The history of the modern theatre, therefore, is not limited by historical specificity but rather can be accessed through different nodal points of interconnection. My approach here is to explore these interfaces through selected plays and their performance histories under the thematic headings of people's history; theatre at the limits of history; romance, rebellion and revolutionary violence; and finally the role of women in challenging colonial, racist, fascist and patriarchal systems.

1 People's History as People's Theatre

That day, piercing through
The fog of the winter of Forty-six
And the darkness of captivity,
Crushing, as if, a tyrant's prison
Rebellious *Khyber* had triumphed
Across the fathomless waters of
The Arabian sea and landed
On the port of Bombay.
[. . .]

The people of great India
Responded to the call at sea,
The streets of the city Kolkata
Filled with roars of waves.

The blue sea was turned incarnadine
By the blood of the men of sea,
Will you avenge the debt of our blood,
They seem to ask us from afar.[1]

This song, sung in powada, a Maharashtrian poetic form which celebrates heroes, tells how the armed workers of Bombay stood with the sailors of the rebel ship *Khyber* of the Royal Indian Navy (R.I.N) to throw off the yoke of imperial exploitation and asks listeners if they would repay this debt of blood to ensure their independence. The song was part of the music score of *Kallol* (Sound of Waves, 1965), a play on the R.I.N mutiny of 1946 written by Utpal Dutt and produced by the LTG at Minerva.

Kallol signalled a new political phase in Dutt's theatre because its politics relied on exposing the limitations of democratic struggle. Dutt developed this genre of plays to argue that Indian independence was not an outcome of widespread Gandhian non-violent movement, but rather a result of the cumulative effect of militancy. The stagecraft of *Kallol* borrowed from the naturalist traditions of the Soviet people's theatre movement, which itself functioned within the aesthetic of socialist realism, epitomized by the Moscow Art Theatre. The role of the 'people' as protagonist in *Kallol*, enjoyed popular success because it reignited 'militant demonstrations of solidarity with the RIN mutineers' in the urban working class and the urban petty-bourgeois and poor (See Figure 4), two decades after the actual event (Guha 1982: 3). As Ranajit Guha has argued, elite nationalist historiography is incapable of accessing such popular militancy as it lurks below the surface of elite colonial parliamentary politics. Dutt was revisiting rebellions as grand spectacle and compelling his audience to reflect on the fragmented histories of such events in terms of their own contemporary time.

Sudipta Kaviraj argues, in *The Unhappy Consciousness: Bankim Chandra Chattopadhyay and the Formation of Nationalist Discourse in India* (1995), that narratives of history and fiction intersect with each other in a fundamental way once historiography becomes the principal concern because 'history instead of being distinguished by the trueness of the story, is now distinguished by the storyness of its truth' (Kaviraj 1995: 107). This process, Kaviraj continues, constructs imaginary history where the past is reconstructed not only

---

[1] Translation of the Bangla text is done by Sayandeb Chowdhury.

Figure 4 A pamphlet published by Little Theatre Group on the popular success of Kallol

through what actually happened but also what might have happened. Crucially, this imaginary history recalls the emotions that might have been at play in deciding the course of an event, including what alternative outcomes might have been possible if emotions had moved in a different direction. This imaginary history is explored from a different angle in Nandi Bhatia's work on Dutt's play *Mahavidroha* (The Great Rebellion, 1973) where Bhatia shows how, on the one hand, Dutt is restoring the rebellion of 1857 into the history of anti-colonial uprisings and rescuing it from its depiction in the colonial archives and nineteenth-century popular British press as 'a horrible, violent and excessive revolt against the British men, women and children' (1999: 176). On the other hand, he is also reflecting on the violent and volatile sociopolitical context of West Bengal in the 1960s and 1970s – rife with popular demonstrations against the government and the Naxalbari movement. Bhatia's analysis traces how Dutt creates heroes from the ordinary people of India as well as his skilful deployment of women characters who challenge traditional representations of Indian women as chaste and passive, thereby making gender an inalienable category for imagining the Indian nation. Drawing from Kaviraj and Bhatia, I would like to explore in this section Dutt's reframing of revolutionary movements in colonial India and internationally as people's history and to test his claim in *Towards a Revolutionary Theatre*, that he always endeavours to put revolution into historical perspective and that this historical perspective is continuously informed by the postcolonial contemporary.

The Postcolonial Conditions of People's History and People's Theatre

People's history connotes an imagination of history beyond the cut-and-dried academic history of text books but does not shun archives as a principal sources for bringing history closer to people's lives. In fact, people's history expands the meaning of archive and attempts to write 'history from below' by using various traces and markings of the passage of time in cultures of orality, performances and visuality, creating multiple narratives of the past. For Raphael Samuel, such an approach may subordinate the 'political' to the 'social' and 'cultural', where political explicitly refers to the state, wars waged by the state and conquests achieved in the name of the state (1981: xv–xvi). The realm of the 'social' and 'cultural', thus conceived, includes engagements with norms, institutions and activities that are not subsumed by the state. However, if we agree, following Samuel, that the 'people' in people's history varies according to its spatial and temporal contexts, it is important to remember that both the social and the cultural can involve politics and even the state in certain contexts (1981: xxi).

In the context of postcolonial history, people's history cannot exclude the 'political' or subordinate it under the 'social' or 'cultural' precisely because people's participation in politics is already denied under the rubric of the 'state' by colonial domination. Elite historiography has for the longest time accounted for such participation as either a 'law and order problem' a 'response to individual charisma' or a 'manipulation of factions' by the colonial and indigenous authorities. While defining a politics of the people in colonial India, Ranajit Guha contends that:

> ... parallel to the domain of elite politics there existed throughout the colonial period another domain of Indian politics in which the principal actors were not the dominant groups of the indigenous society or the colonial authorities but the subaltern classes and groups constituting the mass of the labouring population and the intermediate strata in town and country – that is, the people. (1982: 4)

Guha also reminds us that unlike elite mobilizations, which followed the colonial British parliamentary system and residual semi-feudal political organizations, people's mobilization relied on older networks of kinship, territorialism and class associations, and moreover tended to be more violent in nature because the model for such mobilizations was peasant insurgencies. Even when the urban poor and urban working classes led such mobilizations, the model of peasant insurgencies persisted because it involved a more horizontal form of mobilization against elite domination in all its forms.

The people, as defined in Indian people's history, had entered the stage via the Indian People's Theatre Association, which declared from the outset that 'people's theatre stars the people'. Its first Bulletin in July 1943 stated:

> In recent years, the depth and sweep of the titanic events of contemporary history, the grim brutality of the Fascist attacks on culture and freedom, the grave perils of the present and the prospects of a bright future if reaction is defeated, have all compelled many sensitive writers and artists to realize in varying degrees that art and literature can have a future only if they become the authentic expressions and inspirations of the people's struggles for freedom and culture. (Pradhan 1979: 127)

Modes of authentic expressions in the people's struggle ranged from songs, dances, drama, art and literature, where both folk and classical forms could interact as living traditions, eventually paving the way for people's art forms at their contact zones. Theatre was an important part of this new cultural movement. Its immediate, almost tactile facility for interacting with the masses was recognized by the cultural as well as the political leadership of the Indian communist movement. The new theatre movement, consequently, incorporated culture and politics within its remit from the beginning under the rubric of political theatre which was explicitly designed to represent people's history.

The considerable body of scholarship that already exists on IPTA shows that the revolutionary vision of theatre-workers in the movement involved thinking about the scenography, music, sound and acting style in ways that were completely different from the commercial stage (Bhattacharya 1983; Bhatia 2004; Dutt and Munsi 2010; Singh 2011; Patnaik et al. 2017). As the imperative was to reach as many people as possible, it became crucial to think creatively about what would suit revolutionary aesthetics and be popular at the same time. Conceptual inspiration came from various sources including the Theatre Libre in France, the Independent Theatre in England the Soviet theatre movement at the Moscow Arts Theatre and the Chinese People's Theatre. Theatre workers read Stanislavski, Romain Rolland and Hauptmann and whatever little they could find by Brecht (Roy 2014: 228–230). Close attention was also paid to Indian folk forms and their efficacy in enabling a rethink of stagecraft for the new productions. In Bengal productions ranged from translation of Clifford Odets' *Waiting for Lefty* (fist produced by Bengal Provincial Students'

Federation in 1941), to short propaganda plays like Sukanta Bhattacharya's *Japanke Rukhte Hobe* (Resist Japan), to Rabindranath Tagore's *Rather Rashi* (The Rope of the Chariot) and several plays on the lives of the peasantry like Bijan Bhattacharya's *Jabanbandi* (The Attestation) and Manoj Basu's *Natun Prabhat* (The New Dawn) (Roy 2014: 230–234).

The greatest theatrical triumph of IPTA, *Nabanna* (The New Harvest), first staged at Srirangam theatre in Calcutta in October 1944, follows the fate of a peasant family in the village of Aminpur through the impact of World War II, the disastrous effects of a cyclone, and the ravages of poverty and famine. The episodic structure of the play reflects the perceived need to move beyond naturalistic impulses to represent the intersections of multiple trauma, which could not be contained within a single cause and effect narrative. *Nabanna* made a serious effort to unsettle the conventions of slice-of-life drama. Portraying the unspeakable horrors of famine as a series of episodes, in a nod to Brecht, it was a landmark production not because of its theme, but also because of its use of space, its minimalist approach to props, light and music, and its emphasis on specific dialects. It enjoyed immense success among audiences from various sociocultural backgrounds.

The people's theatre movement suffered massive losses in late 1940s because of internal divisions in the Indian communist movement and Communist Party of India was banned by the Indian government from 1948 to 1952. Cracks had appeared in the leadership and the rank and file between radicals and moderates and increased state repression in the form of police raids of their productions and the invocation of the infamous 1876 Dramatic Performances Act diminished its capability. By the early 1950s the people's theatre movement had begun to transmogrify into the Group Theatre movement as independent theatre groups took forward the legacy of the people's theatre movement in their own ways, interpreting the concept of 'people's theatre' largely within the ideals of the cultural left. However, trained in the tradition of political theatre favoured by IPTA, although his active membership was brief, Utpal Dutt had identified political theatre as his principal art form with people's history as its main narrative focus. All three plays, discussed in this section, are examples of his bringing people's history to stage as people's theatre.

Kallol (Sound of Waves), (1965): A Grand Spectacle with Revolutionary Content

Dutt originally wrote *Kallol* in 1956, after he acquired details of the court martial of the rebellious sailors (Ghosh and Dutt 1991). Initially conceived as a court-room drama, it was revised when LTG realized it needed a spectacular production to draw audiences. After taking the decision to rewrite, a small group from LTG went to the Waterfront Bustee in Bombay for nearly six weeks and interviewed many of the surviving sailors who had gone to prison, had lost their jobs and suffered for participating in the mutiny. Based on these sources the content of *Kallol* was reshaped to reflect on the nature of the struggle, the human relationships amongst the sailors in the ship *Khyber* and their families living in Waterfront Bustee, the contradictions within the leadership of the mutiny, the role of the Indian National Congress and the repressive mechanisms of the British Admiralty. The production design of *Kallol* was directly influenced by the Soviet people's theatre movement which had made a deep impression on Dutt, his set-designer Suresh Datta and his composer Hemanga Biswas.

Dutt and his wife, actor Sova Sen, visited Soviet Union for the first time in 1961. Sen, who played a key female character in *Kallol*, wrote in her memoirs about the impact of watching director Nikolai Okhlopkov's productions *Ocean* and *Thunderstorm* at the Mayakovsky and Mali Theatres in Moscow, as well as about their conversations with the director. To quote from Sen,

> As soon as we sat in the theatre, I noticed that there is no curtain on the stage. A thick blue curtain was laid out on the huge open stage. Slowly the lights started dimming. Suddenly we saw six or seven actors, wearing sailor's costume, came on stage and picked up different sides of that blue cloth. Then they started moving. Gradually they picked up speed. We could feel that waves of turbulent sea were swaying the entire stage. It is difficult to write how mesmerizing it was. Then we saw lights from ships in the distance. We watched the show spellbound. (2017: 62)

Dutt himself confirmed on many occasions that his theatre was immensely impacted by Okhlopkov. In one interview with Surojit Ghosh in *All India Radio* (Dutt 1991), he noted that the emotional depth of Okhlopkov's theatre, even without understanding the language of the play, appealed to him. The quality of compassion in Okhlopkov's theatre could bring tears to the eyes of his Russian audience and for a foreigner like Dutt – the scale of this compassion became inspiring.

Okhlopkov's vision of the deep interplay of colorful emotions is evident in this extract from 'From the Producer's Exposition of Hamlet' (1966):

> Nothing is alien to Hamlet: neither profound depression, nor uncertain gropings towards possible transitions to a life of action, nor despair, nor pessimism; nor yet faith, unlimited faith in the future, in the living springs of life. He is gifted with genuine impetuosity of heart and the passionate temperament of the Renaissance. He knows little, and much. There is much bitter, Voltairian

irony in him, and much that is childishly tender and naïve: a delicate pastel, the subtility of water colour, and the bold oils of high tragedy. (Okhlopkov 1966: 189)

This painterly approach – matching colors and textures with the range of emotional states – was thoroughly imbibed by Dutt. In the opening scene of *Kallol* the sailors are shown as faceless filthy men trapped in the boiler room of a creaking warship, rarely recognizable as individuals. In the second scene, after the sailors become mutineers against the exploitative British navy, they emerge in their white uniform one after another onto the deck where they are transformed into revolutionaries, rediscovering their self-hood with a clear vision of the struggle ahead. The emotional complexity, expressed through the contrast between filth and cleanliness, dark and white in these two scenes of *Kallol*, chimes with Okhlopkov's reflections on the many hues of Hamlet's emotions. Dutt has also spoken in detail about his time spent in front of renowned paintings across Europe and India to contemplate the significance of colour in staging emotion as accurately as possible (2014: 67–69).

For Suresh Datta, training at the Soviet puppet theatre under Sergei Obraztsov, who was the principal artist in setting up Moscow Puppet Theatre in 1960–1961, also proved to be key to designing and building the *Khyber* on the Minerva stage. Suresh Datta had learnt the building miniatures as well as became an expert in using shadows on stage. Datta – along with Dutt and Tapas Sen, the light-designer – went to the shipyards in Calcutta to research the interiors of vessels, in order to make the set as accurate as possible. The result of Datta's meticulous design and craftsmanship was a spectacular warship (See Figure 5), which, with Tapas Sen's light and Biswas's music score the audience's experience of witnessing the lives and struggles of the mutineers. Biswas had been an activist in the new cultural movement initiated by IPTA since 1940s and was working at the Soviet Information Office during the production of *Kallol*. He borrowed songs of the Petrograd naval mutiny of 1917 and Kiel mutiny of 1918 to create a musical architecture of naval songs which he then fused with local Maharashtrian forms to create an international configuration.

The action in *Kallol* moves principally between two locations – the warship *Khyber* and the Waterfront Bustee – with a few scenes at the headquarters of the British Admiralty in Bombay. In the first head-quarters scene, Dutt introduced his comic villains as a double-act. The characters of Admiral Ratrey and the Indian National Congress negotiator Maganlal Jajodia were played through dialogues and gestic articulations infused with satiric humour. Their interactions also serve as exposition. They reveal British suspicion of Soviet Russian involvement in the mutiny because Indian communists are taking

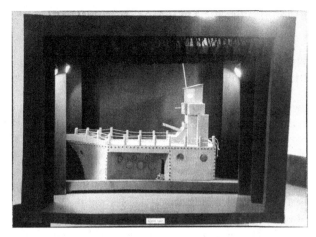

Figure 5 Miniature Model of the ship Khyber in Kallol.

a leading role, the strategy to crush the mutiny by making false promises to the Congress-aligned leadership and to provoke the supporters of democratic struggle to isolate *Khyber* from the rest of the mutineers, and finally, the plan to mow down all resistance at the Waterfront Bustee with armed forces. This last scene becomes particularly crucial in rupturing the elite historiography of Indian nationalism as Dutt mocks Gandhian non-violence and exposes the coalition between British and Indian capitalists as part of the transfer of power.

This rupture becomes an articulation of full-fledged alternative revolutionary truth when betrayed and isolated, the crew of the *Khyber* refuses to surrender even at the cost of death. For Bharucha, this injunction to fight to the end is a distortion of historical fact because the RIN mutineers did in fact surrender. 'Dutt is notoriously contemptuous of facts unrelated to the social turmoil of the working class and their participation in the class struggle', he notes reprovingly (Bharucha 1983: 70). For Dutt, however, such facts represent bourgeois truth because the historical facts of surrender should not occlude the revolutionary truth of the mutiny as the 'beginning of a revolutionary process that . . . set India ablaze with rebellion' (Dutt 2009: 64). Dutt later draws a parallel with Sergei Eisenstein's *Battleship Potemkin* (1925) to explain how revolutionary art considers historical facts within a larger historical perspective and not in isolation. The context of the Russian revolution in October 1917 explains Eisenstein's choicee to end his film at the point of defiance by the rebels, and not to include their final surrender. Thought of in this way, *Kallol* is people's history, I would like to argue, not only because it ruptures elite historiography, but also because it purposefully broadens historical perspectives on Indian nationalism and reframes it as people's history marked both by violent uprisisings, and the solidarity of the masses with such moments.

Ajeya Vietnam (Invincible Vietnam), (1966): Taking Sides in a History of Violence

Noted theatre critic Samik Bandyopadhyay said in an interview with Suchatana Banerjee (2017) about the opening scene of *Ajeya Vietnam*:

> It starts with Dutt as an American general facing the audience and a group of lower-level military men facing him, in almost a classroom situation. Dutt with a stick and board, and there is a map of South East Asia on the board. Then at one point, the screen comes down upon the board and the map magnifies, and Dutt, talking about the importance of American intervention in Vietnam, using his stick points at the map. At one point, he uses the map to point out different geopolitical forces at play, acquainting the audience with the political context – making it very theoretically detailed. Very slowly the lights are dimming and shadows start looming over. For the first time he raises his voice when he goes into rhetoric – and shouts that it is here we will have to contain communism for the whole world. And immediately the stage goes absolute dark, a loud music comes in and through the music the audience sees the drone of flights and then the music fades and the drone take over. Then we have a documentary film clip of bombing – for five minutes – then in a flash full lights come out and the stage shifts into a battle-field hospital with blood dripping, bandaged soldiers, nurses running – right into the middle of a medical camp.

This description captures the immediacy of the spectacle. Dutt put specific emphasis on music to create the ambience for armed struggle for justice. Initially he selected a Vietnamese song to open the play, but during the dress rehearsal realized the song was inappropriate for the mood. 'The theme of the song was something like this – in a war-torn country, a Vietnamese poet is seeking solace in the love of Buddha' he reflects 'but that was not the reality of Vietnam' (Dutt 1994). The clinical clarity with which the American general explains the situation was better supported by ambient music and Dutt finally selected a section of Dmitri Shostakovich's *Leningrad Symphony* (1941) which contains an atmosphere of fears and terror having been written during the Nazi invasion of the Soviet Union.

Bandyopadhyay argues that through this strategy Dutt, very consciously, locates Vietnam's political and historical context in a different idiom. For Bandyopadhyay, Dutt's theatre, gestures towards 'a sort of documentary the-atre' with facts and information, a materially embedded way of representing reality. The status of the claim to truth in documentary theatre, however, is not as secure or straightforward as it may at first appear. Recent scholarship has shown that the form no longer attempts to compel the audience to become a witness to the unimpeachable objective truth of an event or a person but is just as likely to question the value-neutrality of any given document, exploring the dynamism between objective and subjective standpoints – the affect and effect – involved in making sense of the past (Forsyth and Gregson 2009). This inter-rogative strand of documentary theatre is important for shedding light on Dutt's use of facts and information because his plays always perform an active engagement with what he has termed as 'revolutionary truth'. In *Ajeya Vietnam*, scenes involving the torture of a Vietnamese nurse and doctor by American soldiers have repeatedly raised questions about the ethics and aes-thetics of documenting such violence in theatre.

In the opening scene, the American general Fitz-Coulton explains 'Methods of Interrogating Viet Prisoners' which are essentially instructions for torture (1995: 167). For Rustom Bharucha, in what he terms this 'embarrassingly propagandist' play, the details of torture (with hunting knife, barbed wire, butt of the rifle, flamethrower and electric shock) are narrated straightforwardly to emotionally rouse the Bengali audience (1983: 75). In the third scene the Vietnamese nurse Nguyen Thi Mao was gang-raped and then electrocuted to death for concealing information about a Vietnamese guerrilla unit. As these atrocities are committed, the stage is dark, and only sporadically lit by a moving searchlight. During the rape, the only Black signaler among the Americans mechanically sends out a radio message of their location to another American troop. Later, while she is being tortured, the Vietnamese doctor Van Vinh recites poetry.

Bharucha notes in his discussion of the play that Dutt had a tense exchange of words with an American journalist – Mr. Clark from *New York Times* – backstage after a performance of *Ajeya Vietnam* about the impossibility of such American atrocities (1983: 74). Clark, apparently, confronted Dutt about veracity of reports of American soldiers killing unarmed Vietnamese people and Dutt replied that he took it from a newspaper published from Hanoi. For Bharucha, Dutt's willingness to trust a communist Vietnamese newspaper is evidence of his willingness to manipulate the truth in support of Vietnamese propaganda. However, James V Hatch, an American journalist with *New York Times*, who visited Calcutta in the summer of 1968, arrives at rather different conclusions:

> When I saw the mutilation of the girl's breast in his play *Victory Vietnam* I shook my head in disbelief. Yet when I saw the photographs of the girl and read the account in a book how a GI had mutilated her, I accepted it. Dutt faces the problem of verisimilitude. Lies are easier to believe than fact. Who would believe an American boy would cut off a girl's breast wantonly? Most Asians. (Hatch 1968: 7)

Hatch's admission that most Asians would believe in American atrocities acknowledges the long history of support for the Vietnamese struggle in

Bengal. Samik Bandyopadhyay notes that students had marched in Calcutta since the Vietnamese struggle against French colonialism in the 1940s and that this history of association continued well into the late 1960s. Arguably the most spectacular demonstration of leftist student organization in West Bengal was the massive mobilization against the visit of the World Bank president Robert McNamara in Calcutta in November 1968. The Communist Party of India (Marxist) (CPI-M) and the All India Co-ordination Committee of Communist Revolutionaries (AICCCR) organized a combined response. McNamara was described as a 'war-monger' who committed war-crimes against the people of Vietnam, and as a 'neo-colonialist' strategizing to spread 'American imperialism' in India, by Leftist journals – *Ganashakti* and *Deshabrati*. These activities evidence the willing engagement of Bengali youth with the radical politics in 1960s. Moreover, their protest against 'American Imperialism' in 1968 chimed with international student movements in France, anti-Vietnam War protests in the USA, and various Leftist radical movements in Latin America, and Asia (Halliday 1969: 287–326; Jameson 1984).

The people's participation in popular anti-Vietnam war demonstrations also ensured that people's theatre resonated with people's history. The ways in which *Ajeya Vietnam* was recreating people's history on stage could cross borders despite allegations that Dutt was using formulaic stereotypes to portray Vietnamese heroes and American villains. Rustom Bharucha's unease with Dutt's representation of all Vietnamese people on stage as 'fearless, intensely patriotic, and vigorous soldiers, [who are] endowed with all kinds of "civilized" virtues generosity, genial humor, respect for old people, even an affinity for Western classical music and Walt Whitman' and conversely of all Americans as uncouth sadists who torture and kill, taking pleasure from violence (1983: 74) was mildly echoed in a Bengali theatre critic's observation that the play does not represent truth properly (Mancha Rasik 1966). It is worthwhile returning to Hatch's report in this regard because Hatch spotlighted Dutt's commitment to people's theatre by pointing to the fact that Dutt's dramaturgy is melodramatic because it is intended to reach a mass audience. It is important to remember, however, that melodrama is not referred in this case as a lesser form of theatre but rather to highlight Dutt's deft use of larger-than-life emotions to connect with the largest number of people. Hatch's interview with Dutt was tense because the journalist's admiration for Dutt's production was overshadowed by Dutt's stance against American imperialism. 'The American officials in India must wish that Dutt was on our side' Hatch concludes, witnessing 'the dedication of the man and the Little Theatre Group, I wish we were on his' (1968: 7)

Titu Mir (1978): The Making of a People's Hero

When Dutt wrote and produced *Titu Mir* with his group People's Little Theatre (PLT) in 1978, his aim was most probably to revive the staging of historical moments of peasant insurgency in people's theatre. As noted in my Introduction, the play is about the Islamic religious reformer Titu Mir, who organized and led a peasant rebellion from 1827 to 1831 in the Barasat region of Bengal (Dasgupta 1983). The significance of reviving a nineteenth-century Muslim peasant leader as a people's hero only became clear in later productions of the play during periods of communal tension and Islamophobia. For example, *Titu Mir* was revived by PLT, a few months after the destruction of Babri mosque by Hindutva forces in December 1992. Dutt took part in the decision to revive the play as a protest, but unfortunately, passed away in August 1993. *Titu Mir* was again revived in August 2019 by an ensemble group, Theatre Formation Paribartak, when the right-wing government was re-elected for a second consecutive term and Hindutva had become pervasive. The play reflects Dutt's effort to amalgamate *Jatra* with regular proscenium theatre, and was again designed to appeal to the masses, to educate them about histories of subaltern heroes.

Dutt's reflections on the effectiveness of *Jatra* as a vigorous and immediate form, as already mentioned, allows us to think about the appeal of popular theatre in making people's history a part of people's theatre. Dutt stated, quite frankly, that he could not have written *Titu Mir* without his first-hand experience of the impact of *Jatra* on its audience. A fusion of *Jatra*/theatre, he developed it in an effort to create a specifically Indian myth about the historical conditions that had produced religious warriors who opposed imperialism, again educating the masses about their own history.

The scenography of the 1993 production embodied the fusion as it covered a part of the stage with a tent-like structure alluding to the famous bamboo-fort of Titu Mir in Narkelberia village of Barasat (See Figure 6). The costumes also reflected the blending of forms with a somewhat muted version of the usually extravagant *Jatra* costume and a white skull-cap prominently placed on the titular character's head to underline the Islamic context of the rebellion. Dutt himself took the role of Crawford Pyron, an agent of British East India Company and the principal antagonist, in the original production in 1978, Pyron was one of his favourite roles, because in it he could explore the complexities of a scholarly Orientalist British administrator of the nineteenth century, who also personified the diabolical urge to establish British imperialism in India (2014: 72). In the 1993 revival Satya Bandyopadhyay took the role of Crawford Pyron, while Sameeran Choudhury took the role of Titu Mir, subsequently replaced by Dutt's old time actor-collaborator, Samir Mazumdar. It is important to remember the names of actors like Satya Bandyopdhyay and Samir Majumdar because they have been quite central in Dutt's writing of characters in his plays. Dutt often wrote while keeping in mind the skills of the actors in his group (Dutt 2023).

It is perhaps useful to note at this point that Titu Mir was already a controversial figure because of his association with Wahhabi, a conservative orthodox Islamic sect which had been linked to militarized activism in the recent past been characterized as a 'terror' threat. The history of Arabian followers of Muhammad Ibn Abdul Wahab (1703–1792) who put greater emphasis on consulting the *Quran* and *Hadith* directly in everyday life, and the ways Wahhabism spread in South Asia following Syed Ahmed Barelwi (1786–1831) is more complex than a simple history of Islamic fanaticism. Titu Mir, whose actual name was Mir Nisar Ali (1782–1831), was a disciple of Syed Ahmed Barelwi, a Wahhabi leader. Dutt resolves the problem of alleged religious fanaticism by creating a 'proletarian myth' with mass appeal.

The particular qualities of Titu Mir's leadership and the insurgency he led, began to be recognized as a peasant rebellion and not only as a religious uprising in the 1960s (Roy 2012 [1966]). Dutt's play refers to a range of source materials cited in the historiography of Barasat rebellion. These include, Colvin's *Report to the Judicial Department* in 1832 and *The Dampier Report*, from Proceedings

Figure 6 Titumir, People's Little Theatre, 1993

of the Judicial Department in 1847, W. W Hunter's *The Indian Mussalmans* (1876) and O'Kinealy's *The Wahabis in India* (1870) (Dutt 1998: 299–304). As this level of research would imply, Dutt's interpretation closely follows factual details available in the archive, but he succeeds in infusing this archival data with a sense of urgency. *Titu Mir* focuses on a narrative of revolutionary resistance to colonialism and exposes how peasant rebellions involving the rural Muslim dispossessed were marked by the British as instances of Wahhabi religious fanaticism. Julia Stephens has argued that The Great Wahhabi Case (1869–1871) in India, instituted the figure of the Wahhabi religious fanatic precisely to enable the establishment of British authoritarian governance in the colonies (Stephens 2013: 22–52). The Calcutta-based Hindu middle-class succumbed to this British invention due to sustained propaganda in the print media against peasant rebels. Both Biharilal Sarkar's biography of Titu Mir (1897) and Kumudnath Mallik's history of the Nadia district *Nadia-Kahini* (1911) branded the Barasat rebellion an anti-Hindu communal riot.

Dutt's commitment to political theatre as part of the larger Marxist project of revolutionary change is an important lens through which to assess the worldview of Titu Mir. In particular, Dutt's reading of Antonio Gramsci's work enables his conceptualizing Titu Mir as an insurgent subaltern. In his reading of nineteenth-century playwright Dinabandhu Mitra, who had written the play *Nil Darpan* (1859) on peasant revolts, Dutt defined Mitra as a subaltern author who supported peasant insurgency and quoted from Gramsci to introduce his readers in Bengal to this Gramscian term (Dutt 2014: 232). This allows him to revise Marx's own description of the Barasat rebellion as a 'bloody fight between Moslem fanatics under Titu Mir and Hindus' which the British put down (Marx 1947: 129). Dutt's critical revision of the historical context within which Marx was interpreting Titu Mir's Barasat rebellion, reveals the mechanisms by which colonialism localizes such events. Even Marx was fooled. His reading was a product of the 'contemporary' in the nineteenth century, while Dutt's engages with his own 'contemporary' times by revisiting historical moments of peasant rebellion through the prism socialist visions of justice and equality in the Asian contexts of the Chinese revolution in 1949 and the Vietnam War. The play excavates Titu Mir's effort to awaken his people with his own vision of the world, with the sense of a just society that the Company denies the people. The power sought by peasant leaders like Titu Mir did not conform to the ideals of a national secular postcolonial India, but their political activism depended on modes of linking the local with the 'outside'. Dutt frames the politics of the people in terms of peasant consciousness to understand a worldview that is different from the colonial imagination of governance.

This idea of difference is the key to understanding the proletarian mythical hero Dutt was attempting to create in his *Jatra*-theatre. 'A myth' Dutt writes while explaining the inability of modern playwrights to create proletarian myths 'is an intensified, poetic expression of a whole era and therefore true for every era' (2009: 162). Specific and yet timeless, the proletarian myth on stage must release a fierce energy to appeal to every kind of audience and the proletarian hero must embody the challenges of that temporal tension. *Titu Mir* provided Dutt with such myth material. In it, religious warriors wearing the blue of Muslim fakirs could wage a time-specific yet eternal battle against evil, especially imperialism, the greatest evil of all. Religion, in such contexts, could transcend the narrow boundaries of fanatical belief-systems and become a form for embodying the sacred revolutionary duty of resisting imperialism (Guha, 1982).

The character of Titu Mir came to signify the people's hero, embedded in his own history and yet transcending the limits of his time to call for unity among all who have been dispossessed by British colonial forces. He is larger than life and yet human enough to suffer from self-doubt; he is vengeance personified and yet becomes tired of pursuing battle after battle; he is an Islamic religious reformer and yet protecting the hapless Hindu from the British is his sacred task. In fact, Titu Mir became what Dutt considered the exemplary 'proletarian hero' – a hero who alongside his people, and not as an individual 'fights his battles – with the enemy and with himself, to make himself a better fighter and a better man' (1971: 229). The eventual martyrdom of Titu Mir is not imagined as the end of resistance because, for Dutt, the death of a proletarian hero signifies the release of a tragic passion that will raise future warriors. The final lines resonate with Dutt's particular vision of a revolutionary political theatre:

> But, one day there will be soldiers [. . .] Titu Mir is dying with this belief that those who toil every day in this beautiful fertile Bengal, those Hindus and Muslims, will become uncompromising valorous soldiers one day. (Dutt 1998: 362).

Portraying the hero with limitations set by his contemporary times, works to make audience members realize that proletarian heroes are not infallible stereotypes but instead, like them, have foibles and striving to overcome them. Titu Mir could become a people's hero in a proletarian myth because his eventual death was not the end of resistance but rather the beginning of even fiercer battles in which the hero would mature as part of his people.

In conclusion, I would like to draw attention to two issues. The first one concerns Dutt's own evolution as a political artist of Bengali theatre and the second one concerns my efforts to understand how his revolutionary political theatre contributed to the process of decolonization, especially in relation to the environment of cultural politics. The two issues are, in fact, intertwined.

Kallol was not only a spectacle but also an important process of identifying the true revolutionaries who fought against the British colonialism and the nationalist forces who were ready to compromise the struggle in support of the emerging national capitalists. This political process was met with violence when goons, supported by the then ruling government of West Bengal attacked Dutt and other members of his group physically and Dutt was arrested. The play suffered another setback when leading Bengali daily newspapers refused to publish advertisements of *Kallol*. Sova Sen reminiscence about the popular response to such a veritable ban on the play,

> People protested as meetings and protest marches took place spontaneously in support of *Kallol*. Minerva was no more a theatre but rather turned into revolutionary site. People who loved us, who were inspired by *Kallol* came and took our posters to advertise. Tapas Sen created the slogan *Kallol Cholche, Cholbe* (*Kallol* is running and will run). The entire city, railway stations, suburban hamlets and the rural hinterlands started coming up with posters of this slogan. (Sen 2017: 82)

While *Kallol* was running successfully, Dutt felt the need to respond with revolutionary solidarity with the Vietnamese people in 1966. *Ajeya Vietnam* became an extension of Dutt's imagination of 'will to community' for farming-based people of both India and Vietnam. If I borrow from Tony Fisher's argument about the taxonomy of political theatre and think through the fundamental question he raises about the origin of political theatre, it may be possible to see the simultaneous running of *Kallol* and *Ajeya Vietnam* as a larger vision of decolonization across borders in the Global South (Fisher 2023). Together, they represented a shift in Dutt as a political artist who recognized 'the epochal struggle being played out between two antagonistic historical forces' and, in this struggle, his revolutionary theatre found 'a new designation for itself – one that transformed the people's theatre into the vanguard theatre of the proletariat' (2023: 118).

In *Titu Mir* Dutt confronted a different political context from the political life in 1960s West Bengal as the Left Front, a coalition of different communist and socialist parties, won a huge electoral victory in the State Assembly Election in 1977. This was a situation, though much smaller in scale, similar to what Fisher has outlined as the dilemma of Soviet theatre artists immediately after the October revolution in 1917 – to become aesthetically experimental or to remain faithful to the government in power. To borrow terms from Fisher, the distinction was between 'political theatre' that produce social meanings which could be inconvenient for the state and 'governmental theatre' whose ultimate purpose is to suppress critical thought (Fisher 2023: 124). Dutt took the decision, at least it seems from his immediate response after 1977 elections, to return to people's history of peasant rebellion against British imperialism – to continue with the role of vanguard theatre of the proletariat with an emphasis on secularism as a people's ideology in a nation struggling with violent communal tension from its inception in 1947 and to invest in creating a popular culture of taste, a culture of consciousness about struggles ahead.

2 Theatre at the Limit of History: Critical Reflections on Political Theatre

Dutt's understanding of myth and its applicability in theatre is imbued by his understanding of politics – especially his investment in Leftist politics. He traces the larger-than-life quality of myth-making in Shakespeare's plays, referring particularly to monstrous avarice in Iago, Edmund and Claudius; in Goethe's *Faust*; and in the work of Jack London and Ernst Toller. He refers to the character of Mir Jafar – who betrayed the last independent ruler of Bengal, Siraj-ud-Daullah, to Robert Clive, head of the British East India Company in the Battle of Plassey in 1757 – as the 'arche-typal traitor, brilliant in his ambition, intrigue and stupidity', as he is seen in the patriotic play *Siraj-ud-Daullah* (1905) by Girish Chandra Ghose (1844–1912), the most well-known and critically acclaimed actor-director-playwright of the nineteenth-century Bengali stage (2009: 165). In due course, the figure of Mir Jafar came to symbolize betrayal within Indian nationalist discourse.

The construction of a traitor of mythic proportions on stage, because Mir Jafar, even in popular parlance came to be a metaphor of treachery, guaranteed the popularity of early nationalist plays like *Siraj-ud-Daullah*. The influence of such theatre on people's imagination of nationhood could assist in the construction of an anti-colonial political ambience. Mythological plays, drawn from epics like the Ramayana and the Mahabharata, could begin to accommodate a subtext of nationalism because the mythical struggle between good and evil could be immediately associated with colonial domination as evil and nationalist politics as the good. In this way mythological plays became understood as political art in late nineteenth and early twentieth century.

In Dutt's view, however, the petty-bourgeois protagonist of the postcolonial Group Theatre was incapable of carrying the weight of myth – whether bourgeois or proletarian and he laments the absence of a play of mythical proportions in the field of Indian political theatre. He believed that the very trifling everyday struggles of the petty-bourgeois existence disallowed them to be staged in mythical proportions as exceptional class struggle. For Dutt, Tagore's allegorical 1925 play *Raktakarabi* (Red Oleander), which was produced very successfully by the group Bohurupee in Calcutta in 1955, is the closest an Indian political play came in creating a myth.[2] But, in a manner reminiscent of Gorky's inability to give his work a mythical dimension due to his propensity to indulge in the sentimentality of revolutionary romanticism, Tagore is so far away from lived folk-memory that his play becomes submerged in abstract word-play leaving the audience to admire the layers of symbols rather than feel enlivened by its staging of the epic battle between capitalism and labour (Dutt 2009: 165). This absence in postcolonial Bengali theatre compelled Dutt to think through its history, the critical moments of its existence and its political effectiveness vis-à-vis nationalism and decolonization.

This section analyses Dutt's plays *Tiner Tolowar* (The Tin Sword) (1971) (See Figure 7) and *DaNrao Pathikbar* (Stay Passerby) (1980) (See Figure 8) both of which employ the dramaturgical device of play within play and both of which also feature protagonists – real and fictional – from the world of Bengali theatre history and narratives that explore the limits and possibilities of nineteenth-century colonial reformist movements in Bengal. My aim is to shed light on the ways in which Dutt searches for and locates revolutionary truth at the intersections between myth, history and fiction. Dutt was critical and fascinated in equal measure by the reformist achievements of this period. In both plays he explores the limits of the reformers' attempt at modernization. Interestingly, he utilizes women's history, viewed from different perspectives, to address difficult questions of gender equality, women's emancipation and the legacy of colonial modernity, showing how women's bodies became the battleground over which progressive and conservative forces within the colonial intelligentsia fought.

Tiner Tolowar was Dutt's first attempt at exploring this existential crisis and the play became a legend in twentieth-century Bengali theatre history for a number of reasons, including its subject matter, production design, acting and also its overall impact on making theatre an integral part of the decolonization process. Set in 1876 Calcutta, it tells of a theatre group facing severe cash flow problems and in consequently in need of a new play that will make it commercially viable again. Dutt uses dark humour to reflect the historical crisis between colonial modernity and nationalism, which marked this period in Bengal. Women characters, who are actresses within the play, emerge as the principal bulwark in exposing tensions in the colonial bourgeois intelligentsia and commercial collaboration with British colonialism. Passion for theatre, sexual desire, romance and

---

[2] Rabindranath Tagore (1861–1941) was also a playwright and he mostly produced and even performed occasionally in his own plays. He predates the Group Theatre movement in India but his independent productions as well as his distance from the commercial Bengali stage (with a couple of exceptions) makes him accessible to the Group Theatre when it emerged in post-independence India.

Figure 7 Tiner Tolowar, People's Little Theatre, 1971

a nascent nationalist imagination are revealed as deeply gendered as the play progresses through critical moments in the life of the theatre group.

Dutt returned to the same period (1859–1861) nearly a decade later in *DaNrao Pathikbar*, which took as its subject matter a specific moment in the life of the poet and playwright Michael Madhusudan Datta (1824–1873) who was among the most celebrated literary figures of nineteenth-century Bengal. Datta introduced of blank verse into Bengali poetry and in 1861 wrote the epic *Meghnadbadh Kavya* (Slaying of Meghnad). Datta's epic reflects a different take on a particular episode in the Indian epic *Ramayana*, where the demon prince Meghanad is killed in an unjust battle by Lakshman, a human prince and brother of Prince Rama. Datta wrote his epic from the point of view of Meghanad, making him the valorous hero who was betrayed and forced to face Lakshman in an unprepared battle, which underlines Datta's revision of the conventional characterization of the demon prince as a villain. In the play *DaNrao Pathikbar*, Dutt hones in on the period of Datta's preparation for the epic, his forays into amateur Bengali theatre and the flowering of his genius in transforming the Bengali language. *DaNrao Pathikbar* was very well received when it opened at University Institute Hall in Calcutta in January, 1980 and Dutt's portrayal of the protagonist remains one of his towering achievements in acting. The theme of nationalism is explored through several twists and turns, and the Indigo rebellion of 1859 becomes the context for excavating the fraught relationship between colonial education system and popular uprisings.

Patriarchal Chinks in the Progressive Armour of Colonial Modernity

Tiner Tolowar opens with a night scene and a crisis. The Great Bengal Opera, a fictional theatre group in nineteenth-century Calcutta, is preparing to put up a new play, but their heroine, at the eleventh hour, has left them and joined another theatre company. We are introduced to Benimadhab Chatterjee, aka Kapten Babu, the director-playwright as well as the main actor of The Great Bengal Opera, who is out drinking and putting up posters for the new play in different neighbourhoods of the city. The stage space is dominated by a huge poster of the new play *Mayurvahana*, the plot of which, a character in *Tiner Tolowar* later comments, was a clever mixture of the plots of *Hamlet* and *Macbeth* (Dutt 1997: 90). As Benimadhab is admiring it, a scavenger emerges from a manhole stage-right and dumps trash on him. The costumes and language of the scene establishes the period, while the music is derived from the Jatra tradition.

The search for the actress makes *Tiner Tolowar*'s plot gendered from the outset. The first half concerns the search, and once a suitable candidate is found, with her training in language and posture. The second half reveals tensions in the new actress's life via exploration of her relationships with different representatives of colonial patriarchy, who are undergoing conflicting experiences of modernity. In Bengali public theatre actresses were typically drawn from disreputable quarters of the city, a fact which generated anxiety regarding the respectability of theatre itself and also challenged emerging ideals of domestic conjugality and respectable femininity. In *Tiner Tolowar*, this discursive cultural context is explored through two actresses from different generations. Basundhara, the older actress who plays principal women characters in The Great Bengal Opera, comes from the prostitute quarters and has studied stage acting from older maestros of Bengali theatre. Moyna, the younger actress, has an urban working-class background.

The sexual anxiety around Moyna's origin is first glimpsed in the second scene when Beerkrishna Da, the lecherous proprietor of the theatre group, wants to have a look at the new heroine. Benimadhab, with his quick wit, realizes that in order to ensure the funding for his new play from the proprietor he must present Da with a novelty and claims that Moyna is actually a respectable woman from an impoverished family, a ruse supported by his changing her name to the more respectable Shankari. His trick pays off as Da beomes enamoured by the idea of having a respectable actress in his theatre and doles out whatever money Benimadhab needs. Da's fascination enters new territory in a later scene when he offers to sign over the proprietorship of the theatre company to Benimadhab, if Moyna/Shankari agrees to become his exclusive mistress. He insists keeping a 'respectable' mistress would enhance his social status. This particular crisis reveals the patriarchal authority embedded within colonial modernity as Benimadhab readily agrees to Da's offer. Basundhara, however, rebels. The older actress has noticed the blossoming love between Moyna and Priyanatha Mallik, a representative character of the Young Bengal[3] group, and she wishes to fulfil her own thwarted dream of conjugal love vicariously through Moyna.

Benimadhab sheds the persona of a paternalistic patriarch when Moyna decides to leave with Priyanath. He claims every bit of the newly literate, reformed, sophisticated woman Moyna has become is his creation and that she can leave the theatre only after returning those gifts. This monstrous demand is a reminder of the limits of the entire social reform movement of the nineteenth century which sought to create the female counterpart of the emerging gentleman *bhadralok* by reforming and refining apparently 'coarse' and 'vulgar' precolonial ideas of femininity. Basundhara berates Benimadhab, saying that her fate as an aging actress with a disreputable past forces her to stay with The Great Bengal Opera but her faith in its greatness has faded. Her words resonate with the larger tragedy of poor, working-class women of dubious birth, who were bypassed by colonial modernity's project of reforming women. By placing these two women characters in a relationship of tension with Benimadhab, Dutt exposes the irresolvable tensions within the long, revered history of Bengal Renaissance.[4]

Basundhara is the archetypal actress of the nineteenth century, burdened with disreputable origins and reliant on her body as the principal means of earning a living, she is obliged to live a double life, appearing as strong chaste women on public stage while entertaining patrons in private. Moyna, on the other hand, represents the conflicted 'new woman' of colonial modernity who

---

[3] The Young Bengal was a group of radical students of Hindu College in early nineteenth century, who were greatly influenced by their teacher Henry Louis Vivian Derozio (1809–1831).

[4] Bengal Renaissance refers to the nineteenth century 're-awakening' in the social, cultural and political life of colonial Bengal. It included social reform movements like the Abolition of *Sati* (the Act was passed in 1829) and Widow Marriage (the Act was passed in 1856) as well as new energy in the literary field with Bankim Chandra Chatterjee (1838–1894) writing the first successful novel *Durgeshnandini* (1856) in Bengali. Raja Ram Mohun Roy (1772–1833), Ishwar Chandra Vidyasagar (1820–1891) and Rabindranath Tagore (1861–1941) are regarded as doyens of Bengal Renaissance who ushered in modern thinking in the everyday life of Bengal.

suddenly finds her life divided between the mutually exclusive realms of 'home' and the 'world'. She can either become a happy wife or a famous actress but not both. She finally chooses the life of the actress, making the sacrifice of becoming the mistress of Beerkrishna Da and rejecting the hope of domestic bliss with Priyanath. Her self-realization – her ambition to be known, admired and celebrated as an actress – further reveals the contradictions at the heart of the bourgeois myth of the romantic sensuality of the actress. She begins asserting agency over her craft, thereby creating an identity of her own, to the increasing sexual anxiety of middle-class patriarchy. *Tiner Tolowar* explores this tension on stage by highlighting the ways the fraught gender politics of respectability played out amongst leading male director-playwrights, lascivious proprietors and actresses across generations back-stage in the public theatre.

DaNrao Pathikbar also picks up the thread of women's history at this point of transition in lives of actresses. It opens with a performance of a fictional *kheur* – A Bengali folk form of songs with bawdy lyrics – group, led by the female performer Sarayumani. Again, the song establishes the period, but it also reminds the audience about the divide between the amateur theatre of the urban gentry and Sarayumani's group of performers in terms of 'decency' in the imagination of the colonial modern. This tension is worth unpacking further. In his study of the oral subcultures of lower-caste and lower-class women in pre-colonial and early colonial Bengal, Sumanta Banerjee demonstrates that such performances were subversive sites of women's resistance to the emerging *bhadralok* patriarchy (Banerjee 1989). These women, Banerjee shows, engaged in 'disrespectful' professions of sex work and performing arts, mocked *bhadralok* ideals of domesticity, femininity and conjugality through their songs and performances. Such resistance exposed the exclusionary politics of colonial modernity in establishing ethical romantic love as the social ideal.

Dutt challenges exclusionary patriarchal politics by creating a more mutually mobile relationship between feminine oral culture, represented by Sarayumani and elite Bengali literate culture, represented by Michael Madhusudan Datta. In the play Sarayumani gets to listen to some fragments of Michael's Bengali poems and immediately recognizes blank verse as a potential form for her own creations and using it to compose commentary on the Indigo Rebellion among urban and rural people. Dutt develops Sarayumani into a proto-type of a nationalist artist in a scene where she is tortured by an Indigo planter for disseminating words of rebellion. The interplay of cultural forms is not limited to infusing an ostensibly 'lower' folk orality with literate 'higher' forms, in the play. Michael wants a folk-poet to create music for his new social farce and admires Sarayumani's songs about the oppressive Indigo planters when he hears

Figure 8 DaNrao Pathikbar, People's Little Theatre, 1980

them at a street-corner gathering. The 'disreputable' actress finds a supporter in the mercurial genius of the poet.

Dutt's gendered critique of colonial modernity is further anchored in Michael's private life. Dutt creates a scene, early in the play, where the poet is busy writing, and the stage is transformed into the world of his imagination through a change of lighting. As the audience enters his inner world, his first wife, Rebecca McTavish, whom he had abandoned with four children in Madras to live with his mistress Henrietta Sophie White in Calcutta, comes in his conscience to remind him of his cruel desertion, her back-breaking poverty and their incessant disagreements about his extravagant expenses. A very different aspect of the poet character is revealed through this scene, then, and the play refuses to allow Datta's misdemeanours to be overshadowed by his genius as an artist. As the plot progresses, the audience sees that despite Rebecca's presence in his conscience, he has not amended his extravagant habits. On the contrary, his love of finery reaches the extent of starving his own children.

Rebecca, as an embodied presence, inhabits his conscience once more towards the end of the play where he tries to dismiss her by insisting, he has become tired of her efforts to torture him. Her stubborn presence, however, compels the audience to reflect not only on his cruelty but also on a less discussed aspect of the personal histories of the doyens of the Bengal Renaissance. The idea of women's emancipation had only partially entered their private spaces. Rebecca and Michael's interaction within the fictional space of Michael's memory/conscience allows for a glimpse at the darker recesses of colonial modernity: a kind of unkempt and shabby dressing room at the back of a magnificently lit theatre.

Play within Play: Theatre as the 'Dressing-Room' of History

The space and place of theatre has been theorized in various different ways by scholars whose interests range from the precise location of a theatre or theatre district within a city, to the exterior and interior architectural design of theatres, to the ways in which stage space invokes a sense of fictional and historical place (Redmond 1987; Issacharoff 1989; Davis 1991; Reinelt and Roach 1992; McAuley 1999; Solga 2019). The dressing room, or the green room, where costuming of actors take place, and which may or may not double as rehearsal space remains marginalized in these discussions. In fact, as Gay McAuley observes, practitioner space is the least theorized, least analysed and least documented despite the fact that it could offer important insights into practitioners' experiences (1999: 26). The significance, or lack of it, accorded by scholars to this space in terms of the social organization of performance and the effect of this space in shaping the relations with the audiences is not acknowledged (McAuley 1999: 26). Bringing the dressing room on stage is thus vital in articulating the politics of *Tiner Tolowar* and its commentary on the themes it addresses.

The second scene introduces all of the principal characters as they interact. The stage resembles the dressing room of a ramshackle theatre group where everyday objects like kitchen utensils, towels and garments are left alongside spectacular costumes, a throne, costume jewellery, lighting equipment and various headdresses. The actors – of The Great Bengal Opera – are seen rehearsing the new play. By way of exposition, the scene revels the different layers of society involved in the public theatre, and how their relationships are marked by different kinds of contradictions. Priyanath arrives to meet Benimadhab and informs the group, to its incredulity, that he has come to instruct their leader in proper theatre:

> I have learnt theatre from Captain Pendlebury at Hindu College. I have acted in English plays at the San Souci theatre at the Park Street. I have noticed for some time now, how you have been producing ugly and futile plays without any substance. The entire society is facing a crisis and you are busy here creating a false, illusory world of royal romance on stage. (Dutt 1997: 92)

Priyanath then announces that he has written a play which will put an end to this tomfoolery. Based on the Battle of Plassey (1757), in which the British gained control over the Bengal, it will expose Robert Clive as a thug. Priyanath's declaration acts as a critique of the nineteenth-century Bengali stage on two levels. First, proscenium theatre with its undeniable colonial history needs to acknowledge its origin, and learn from the techniques particular to the Western tradition to become better at its principal function: staging engaging plays. Second, anti-colonial themes can be successfully staged through a colonial form, and such an approach can thus create a space for nationalist discourses in theatre. The dressing-room on stage also becomes the dressing room of history, a space marked by the actions of individual actors preparing, however tentatively, for the 'show'.

In this early scene, Dutt begins the work of carefully unpicking the relation-ship between theatre history and the real-life biographies of the doyens of Bengal Renaissance within the larger framework of colonial modernity and nationalist discourse. For instance, he maintains Girish Chandra Ghose as a haunting presence and rival of Benimadhab, while weaving some of Ghose's major characteristics into his characterization of the fictional Benimadhab. Similarly, the earliest generation of actresses from red light areas – Tinkari and Elokeshee – are principal reference points for the character of Basundhara. Priyanath Mallik is a composite of English educated Bengali youth and functions partly as Benimadhab's alter-ego and Moyna is an echo of Binodini Dasi (1863–1941), the most famous actress of this time who registered her defiance in her autobiography *Amar Katha* and *Amar Abhinetri Jiban* (My Story and My Life as an Actress). Moyna becomes a barometer for the limits of the social reform project of Bengal Renaissance. Dutt also gives us the spectral presence of Lambert (*Lambo Saheb*), the Deputy Police Commissioner of Calcutta, a fearsome figure for theatre companies especially after the passing of the draconian Dramatic Performances Act of 1876. Finally, Beerkrishna Da is another composite character personifying the comprador business class which has collaborated with various colonial commercial ventures.

Naming his fictional theatre company The Great Bengal Opera is probably the most obvious marker in defining the historicity of *Tiner Tolowar*. The Bengal Theatre (1873–1901) was the first Bengali public theatre in Calcutta with a permanent stage, and it was followed by Star Theatre (1883), The Great National Theatre (1873 and 1911), National Theatre (1877) and The Grand National Theatre (1911–1914). Dutt reassigns The Great National Theatre to 1876 so that it can serve as a rival for The Great Bengal Opera. The prevalence of the suffix 'national' is significant in this history because, as Nandi Bhatia has pointed out, 'theatre's visual focus, emphasis on collective participation and representation of shared histories, mobility, potential for public disruption and spatial manoeuvrability' allows it to disseminate among the public, whether literate or unlettered, definite nationalist articulations of protest (2004: 3). Repeated references in *Tiner Tolowar* to what The Great Bengal Opera can or cannot produce, which compromises it can or cannot negotiate, and in whose voice it can or cannot speak, spotlights the processes through which public theatre was becoming a part of nationalist politics.

It is important to keep in mind that these historical parallels are being drawn not merely to regale the 1971 audience with a slice of theatre history, but also to remind the public about the critical role of theatre as a weapon for mass mobilization. The play's title obviously resonates with these concerns and draws attention to the effectiveness or otherwise of the tin sword used in stage-fights in engaging with real politics. Dutt's drawing of historical parallels, between 1876 and 1971, occurred within the political milieu of a period in which public theatre was infused with anti-government sentiment, and registered its resistance through the performance of historical and mythological plays that produced serious critique of the colonial regime and its legacies and drew parallels with the current postcolonial government (Chowdhury 2023). Dutt brings in recitations of grand rhythmic dialogues in classical Bengali for The Great Bengal Opera's *Mayurvahana* the play within the play, but uses nineteenth-century colloquial Bengali with generous dollops of period-typical slang in the dialogues between characters. The linguistic texture of the play was augmented by a physical acting style in which certain elaborate gestures of the hands and body marked the historical period in which it was set, by applying them in the play within the play, but also transcended it by bringing in naturalistic gestures outside the 'play within the play' context, to communicate with the postcolonial contemporary. His stagecraft in *The Tin Sword* became a space of continuous dialogue through time, with the use of an orchestra pit, the transformation of two side-windows into old-style boxes. In this way the scenography performed a hundred years of proscenium theatre as a space of lived politics.

The historicity of *DaNrao Pathikbar* is self-evident because its central character Michael Madhusudan Datta was a real person. The ensemble of historical figures – including Ishwar Chandra Vidyasagar (1820–1891), Gour Das Bysack (1827–1899), Reverend James Long (1814–1887) and Jatindramohan Tagore (1831–1908), along with Rebecca Mctavish and Henrietta, and other members of his family – surrounding the central character constitutes the personal, political and social tensions of the time in which they lived. Dutt's fascination with Datta as an illustrative character of the Bengal Renaissance in terms of his daring to think in new ways by trouncing the old structures of beliefs, norms, even literary traditions, means that *DaNrao Pathikbar* emerges as something more than a biographical play. For Dutt, Datta was 'limited by the essential backwardness of the colonial bourgeoisie, but his was by far the most eloquent expression of vacillating bourgeois humanism of his own time' (2009: 163). Moreover, the play resonates with the audience in 1980, because West Bengal was entering a new phase of democracy as the Left Front Government came to power after years of a stifling and oppressive National Emergency[5], possibly because of the irrepressible hope embodied in the character of Datta.

Sarayumani and her *kheur* group are inspired by the acclaimed women performers of the period, and perhaps also to the famous woman *Kabiyal* Jajneswari (dates unknown, Nandy 1957: 105). The folk form *Kabigan* involves a spontaneous repartee of songs on various social themes by two rival poets. Elsewhere in the play, Sudarshan Dutta and Rambishnu Mukherjee are representative of the decadent and conservative upper-caste urban society of Calcutta who opposed Vidyasagar[6] for his reformist activities and derided Michael for his Christianity. Dutt carefully builds the linguistic atmosphere by showing Datta's proficiency in several European languages, Latin and Hebrew as well as in Bengali's regional dialects, which he contrasts with the chaste Bengali of Vidyasagar and Sarayumani's much more colloquial Bengali. Meanwhile, the character of Sudarshan Dutta speaks in grammatically incorrect English to provide comic relief, while also demonstrates his subservience to British colonial rule. The production design and scenography 'almost resembled a commercial theatre' in terms of creating spectacles with light and set, which resulted in more than hundred performances and 'established University Institute Hall as a theatre' (Chattopadhyay 1998: 659). I would like to read the reference to commercial stage more as a mark of appreciation than derision, because the commercial theatre had the resources to create elaborate stage which the funding-starved Group Theatre often lacked. The comparison, I think, reflects Dutt's ability to combine his aesthetic scenography along with fresh sets to appeal to popular taste for refinements in theatre.

Dutt uses the device of the play-within-play in *DaNrao Pathikbar* in an unusual way, to allow the audience to enter Datta's inner world where it encounters his creative genius as well as his troubled conscience. Lighting effects are used to signal the shift from external to internal reality, giving the drawing room in his Calcutta residence a different and more shadowy atmosphere. In the previous section, I referred to this psychic space as a dressing room, an unkempt dark chamber of colonial modernity when Datta is

---

[5] A state of internal emergency was declared by Prime Minister Indira Gandhi in 1975 when every democratic freedom was curtailed in India. The period of emergency continued until 1977.

[6] Ishwar Chandra Vidyasagar is most well known for his relentless struggle to pass the Widow Marriage Act. However, he was also a leading figure in the Bengali literary sphere for shaping the modern Bengali language and as an educationist, he encouraged opening of new schools to teach English language and new scientific education. He was also a pioneer of introducing modern schooling among women of Bengal.

confronted by his abandoned wife Rebecca McTavish. The dressing room is a space where unused or rejected objects, practices and ideas are discarded by practitioners and Datta's troubled conscience becomes a dressing room of history because it contains uncomfortable aspects of the Bengal Renaissance that have been occluded by historians of that period. The interactions between Rebecca and Michael are, of course, taking place inside his head. Nonetheless, during her first appearance Rebecca clearly articulates, what Dutt, considers 'the essential backwardness of the colonial bourgeoisie' by revealing Datta's ambition to emulate English poetry and to live as an European in brown skin (Dutt 2009: 163). Rebecca also reminds him that they are not divorced, so that Henrietta can never be his wife and their children will be illegitimate. 'Yes, I am cruel and selfish', Datta admits, in a moment of confession made possible only by Dutt's purposeful melding of history and fiction (Dutt 1998: 500). Theatre as the dressing room of history, thus, becomes a useful space where unspoken parts of history can find articulation.

Myth, History and Fiction: Situating the Insurgent Subaltern

Let me return to the very first scene of *Tiner Tolowar* to contextualize Dutt's attempt at producing both a bourgeois myth and its subversion. The scavenger dumps trash on Benimadhab, who being a gentle drunk, does not take offence but rather engages him in conversation, trying to understand if his theatre appeals to the person who self-consciously declares *ami Kolketar tolay thaki* (I live at the bottom pit of the city). Benimadhab is then roundly rebuked by the scavenger, who says that his fancy plays with mellifluous words and colourful costumes have nothing to do with the working-class poor. The theatre-maker faces a further challenge when the scavenger asks, 'well, can you leave out those fairy tales about kings and queens, and write a play about me? huh, you Brahmin, you would lose your caste if you try that!' (Dutt 1997: 80). Benimadhab feels the sting in this remark and tries to explain that his caste is mere *theatre-wallah* with no Brahminical association, but all his efforts to argue how he became a theatre person through long experiences in playing at the *jatra* fall on deaf ears. The scavenger keeps dumping trash on him and mocking him with accusations that he and his ilk merely create spectacles with tin swords. This sequence sets the tone of the play and uses humour to expose the huge distance between the common people and the subject matter of Bengali theatre.

However, the revolutionary artist in Dutt takes a final swipe at the public theatre by allowing the disgraced Benimadhab a moment of redemption in the final scene. As a defeated, Benimadhab forces his actors to play an innocuous social farce instead of a nationalist play to an invited audience, said audience jeers at him. Both Moyna and Basundhara tried to reason with him about the pride and honour of The Great Bengal Opera in upholding the uncompromising glory of defiant theatre, and yet Benimadhab persists on compromising with the colonial government. His sudden awakening occurs when he remembers that certain doyens of the public theatre have been imprisoned for protesting against the Dramatic Performances Act, and he decides the company will switch to performing the nationalist play *Titu Mir*, written by the young idealist Priyanath Mallik. Benimadhab utters the famous line – 'the tin sword is now unsheathed' – in the middle of the social farce and in so doing transforms into the principal character in *Titu Mir*. This prefiguration of *Titu Mir* in Dutt's theatre is interesting in itself, but the play within a play in *Tiner Tolowar* is already a weapon for fighting colonial-capitalist oppression, indicating Dutt's vision of the purpose of true political theatre.

The only publicly available audio-visual clip of the production of *The Tin Sword* contains this final act. It opens with Dutt, playing Benimadhab, taking off his costume and adorning the blue robe of Titu Mir while Sova Sen, playing Basundhara, begins to recite the dialogues from Priyanath Mallik's *Titu Mir* play. Chhanda Chatterjee, playing Moyna, from the 'box' up on the left side of the stage, starts signing the patriotic song before descending, assuming her role in *Titu Mir* as Bangalaksmi. The jeering from the audience becomes enthusiastic admiration and the British Deputy Commissioner of Police, Lambert shouts 'You will pay for this! I swear you will pay for this!' (Dutt 1997: 141). The curtain comes down as Dutt playing Benimadhab playing Titu Mir, slays the exploitative colonist McGrear (*Maguar*) with his tin sword. A new nationalist myth of the insurgent subaltern is thus inaugurated in political theatre with actresses flanking the stage as participants in its creation.

In *DaNrao Pathikbar*, the intertwining of history, myth and fiction finds embodiment in the fifth scene, where Datta first encounters Rebecca, drives her away by saying that he is busy with his new creation, and starts reciting the first lines of his famous epic *Meghnadbadh Kavya*. In the beginning of the sixth scene, he is busy in his drawing room, reciting simultaneously to two scribes two different creations, *Brajangana Kavya* based on the Vaishnava theme of love between Krishna and Radha and *Meghnadbadh Kavya*. After a brief exchange with Henrietta on pathos in Vaishnava idea of love, he returns to *Meghnadbadh Kavya*, as she exits. As Michael starts reciting from the epic, the lights change and the audience enters the mind-space, witnessing the creative process in his consciousness. His voice is interrupted by the voice of Major Hodson, the Englishman who retrieved Delhi from the rebels during the Great

Rebellion of 1857.[7] It signals that in Michael's mind, the epic characters from the *Ramayana* are becoming historical characters in the Great Rebellion of 1857 in this additional play within the play.

> Hodson's voice: We shall pave the roads of London with the bones of Indian princes. Shoot him down like a dog.
> Mirza Mughal's voice: This is not the way of men. This is injustice, treachery! [*yeh mard ka tarika nahi. Yeh be-insafi, beyimani!*]
> Nana Sahib's voice: I am taking an oath in the name of blood-soaked Delhi, not a drop of blood of these braves will go in vain.
> [gradually a chamber of the Red Fort in Delhi opens in front of Michael. Meghnad, the demon prince, dressed as Mirza Mughal, a Mughal prince in Delhi is looking up after *Namaz* and is seeing in front of him Laksman, the human prince, dressed as Hodson]. (Dutt 1998: 504)

Hodson/Laksman and Mirza Mughal/Meghnad start reciting their respective dialogues from *Meghnadbadh Kavya* and a duel with swords begin.

Dutt creates a moment of anti-colonial struggle using Datta's characters, making their author a supporter of the rebellion. It is important to remind ourselves what Dutt says about the political nature of Datta's epic:

> Since he [Michael Madhusudan Datta] called himself a disciple of Milton, the half-baked scholars of our country have been busy comparing his blank verse with that of Milton. They attribute a debt of mere form, obliterating the fact that Milton was also the most advanced expression of the armed-bourgeois-democratic revolution in England, and that Michael might have been a similar expression in our barren soil. No one seems to have noticed that the epic on the death of Meghnad may be an attempt to recreate a myth in terms of an armed struggle against oppression [. . .] No one appears interested in the similar cowardly murder of the Prince in Delhi by Hodson, a little before Michael wrote *Meghnadbadh Kavya*. (Dutt 2009: 163)

Writing in the early 1980s, Dutt would have been familiar with the ongoing re-evaluation of the Bengal Renaissance and especially the status of Datta within it, among historians and literary critics of Bengal, which had its roots in the Leftist circles of the mid-1960s. His reading, quite clearly, is not wholly in agreement with those critics who denied its relevance in nationalist discourse, and considered its principal figures largely as collaborators with the British. In the play, Dutt re-asserts Datta's nationalism in the final scene when the French

---

[7] The Great Rebellion of 1857 is often referred in the colonial historiography as the Sepoy Mutiny. The Indian soldiers and Indian princes from northern and western India declared independence from the British East India Company under the leadership of the surviving Mughal emperor Bahadur Shah Jafar in 1857. Delhi became the rebel headquarters. The Company finally quelled the uprising through brute force by the end of 1857. After this rebellion the British crown took over the governance of India from the Company.

police arrests him mistakenly as Nana Sahib, a rebel prince who led Indian soldiers during the Rebellion of 1857 and he had fled when he was defeated by the British. Datta, in the play, welcomes his chains as they allow him, even if under false pretences, to rebel against the colonial forces. In the fictional imagination, as Datta is mistaken for Nana Sahib, the layering of myth and history, which Dutt creates through amalgamating the characters of Hodson/ Laksman and Mirza Mughal/Meghnad, becomes more complex. The question of whether Datta was 'ahead of his time' or 'very much of it' remains a source of debate among literary critics and historians but in Dutt's creation he becomes a palimpsest of political action that rises against oppressive regimes, allowing the audience another glimpse of the coming of the insurgent subaltern to the stage (Chaudhuri 2009).

3 In Love and War: Nationalism and Decolonization in Jatra

The history of modern Indian theatre is often reiterated as a single narrative without regional and/or linguistic variations. Thus, it seems to have been constructed to fit notions of national modernity rather than to reflect the uneven patchwork of multiple, sometimes overlapping and sometimes contradictory, traditions of performance that actually exist (Chatterjee 2016). Returning to regional and linguistically distinct histories of modern theatre would, I suggest, be a more productive way of engaging not only with theatre history, but also with multiple and various modes of writing and performing in their specific locales. A very short tour through the historically relevant details about the folk form of jatra will help us in mapping and unpacking narratives of nationalism and decolonization as they occur in Dutt's foray into this form.

Historians of jatra argue that it became a form of popular entertainment from the sixteenth century in Bengal, principally with the emergence of the narrative form of *Mangal Kavya*, long propitious poems about a deity, connected with a sect or a cult (Sarkar 1975; Ghosh 1996; Pandit 2015). The oral tradition of reciting these poems was turned into audio-visual performances with lyrics and songs that propagated the origin myths of sects/cults and episodes from different faith traditions like *Krishna Jatra* and *Kaliya Daman* in the Vaishnava tradition, *Chandi Jatra* and *Shiber Geet* in the Shakta tradition, *Manasar Bhasan* about the glories of serpent goddess Manasa, and *Ram Jatra* about episodes from the epic Ramayana. The form began to develop distinctive characteristics in nineteenth century as it came in contact with European theatre in the city of Calcutta. Jatra performances began to incorporate social issues but came up with the unique characters of *Bibek* or Conscience and *Niyati* or Nemesis who performed certain choral functions. From loosely connected songs with a tenuous thread of narrative, jatra became a fusion folk-form of play-acting with costumes and make-up, songs with grand gestures played on make-shift stages in the open air and connecting emotionally with its audiences through mimetic connection with the strong flow of narrative (Ghosh 1996: 51–69).

Jatra, from this period, was essentially performed by touring companies or troupes that travelled the rural areas and smaller towns, occasionally performing in the suburban fringes of Calcutta. Principally associated with the *Adhikari*, or director-playwright, who was sometimes also the owner of the troupe, its popularity depended on the fame of the *Adhikari* rather than any particular form-based tradition of performance. In early nineteenth-century figures includ-ing Shishuram Adhikari, Gobinda Adhikari, Badan Adhikari and Lochan Adhikari were notable for their contribution to consolidating jatra as a full-fledged cultural form based on the earlier traditions (Ghosh 1996: 55–60). The significance of the jatra audience has been highlighted by almost every scholar for its contribution to the form's evolution (Sarkar 1975; Ghosh 1996; Das 2005: 241–249; Das 2012; Deb Barman 2014; Pandit 2015). Jatra performances typically catered to audiences of thousands, especially popular plays by a well-known *Adhikari*. The wide reach of jatra made it an object of government surveillance when it began to propagate nationalist themes in the early twentieth century.

During the first anti-Partition agitation in Bengal in 1905 – the Partition of the province proposed by Lord Curzon, depended largely on dividing the popula-tion between Hindu and Muslim communities within specific territories – Mukunda Das (1878–1934) emerged as a strong voice of communal harmony and nationalist emotion in the sphere of jatra. The colonial government took notice of him and others in 1910 because they feared the plays were conveying 'disaffection and hostility towards the established authority' (Pandit 2015: 26). Mimasha Pandit singles out the mythological play or *pala*, as the text of Jatra is often called in Bengali, *Matripuja* (Worshipping the Mother) by Gangan Chandra Sutradhar, with a skit by Mukunda Das as rallying points for the rural populace of Bengal for the anti-Partition movement (2015: 27). It is important to mention here that jatra playwrights were practical enough to present politically charged plays as a mythological ones to attract the attention of the largest number of people and had woven the nationalist message in through a skit where the primordial force (*adya shakti*) could integrate the ideals of the divine warrior mother and express it as the mother nation. Mukunda Das's songs could infuse the audience with emotion that combined devotion of *bhakti* with *deshprem* or patriotism.

Let me pause here and make an effort to connect the ideas of *deshprem* with *prem* (love) in the cultural discourse of nineteenth- and early twentieth-century

Bengal to make sense of performing the emotional politics of love for one's own country. The emotional aspect is important precisely because jatra has been traditionally dependant on moving its audience within an emotional arc, pitched so high, that the audience could easily become immersed in the performance. Sudipta Kaviraj has attempted a conceptual and social history of love in late colonial Bengal through an exploration of modern Bengali literature and its focus on private life in *The Invention of Private Life* (2014). The diversity available in the lexicon of love – *adirasa, shringara, sakhya, vatsalya* in Sanskrit literature; the Islamic traditions of *ishq, muhabbat, ibadat* or even *junoon* (frenzy or excess of love) – had informed eighteenth- and early-nineteenth-century Bengali literature, principally the tradition of poetry. Kaviraj argues that authors and artists of the late nineteenth century zeroed in on *prem* (which was an indeterminate form of love) as the most suitable conceptual framework for describing love and developed it as a definition of ethical romantic love as opposed to physical beauty, eroticism and sexuality (2014: 161–164).

This focus on *prem* is symptomatic of the emergence of *bhadralok* or gentlemen within Bengali society, a figure whose carefully constructed moral universe is based on colonial modernity. The encounter between the cultural politics of colonial modernity and the growth of nationalist political thought defined the cultural practices of this moral universe. The definition of *prem*, as it became associated with *desh* or nation, became a wider field of emotional politics, beyond romantic attachments between individuals and began to cross-over with *bhakti* (devotion). It is interesting note at this point that, though jatra was not associated with the urban, educated *bhadralok*, it could bring in the idea of *prem*, fuse it with the idea of mother nation and disseminate it among its large audience in the language of nationalism as love for one's own country. This particular moment of connection between jatra, nationalist politics and emotional connection with the issue of Partition, consequently, initiated the politicization of jatra, which carried over into the 1960s and 1970s and the period of decolonization.

It is equally important to mention here the specific kind of gender politics that underpinned the organizational form of jatra and had an interesting impact, especially in the period of decolonization, on representing femininities and masculinities on stage vis-à-vis ideals of nationalist politics. Unlike the proscenium theatre, where actresses came to perform from 1870s, the jatra space was dominated by female impersonators until 1950s with a few women dancers travelling with the troupes. In the actor-hierarchy, women began to make their presence felt when actress Jyotsna Dutta's performance, first as a replacement and then regularly, as the leading lady in the play *Sonai-dighi* became a runaway success in the 1958–1959 season (Dutt 2010: 122). Bishnupriya Dutt notes that by the middle of 1960s every touring jatra company had women playing the leading female characters whereas female impersonators had been relegated to playing older women (2010: 123–124). Since this was a crucial shift in the moral economy of jatra, the actress's presence on stage needs to be contextualized in relation to their roles both on and off stage. Patriarchs of the jatra scene like Brajen De, Phani Babu (Boro/elder) and Phani Babu (chhoto/younger) lamented that the entry of women would vitiate the already loose morality of the touring companies, but they could not resist the new public demand for actresses on stage (Dutt 2010: 127–128). To contain the actresses' presence, therefore, different strategies were developed. On stage, plays like *Sonai-dighi* emphasized the chastity, purity and righteousness of young women, creating an aura of middle-class respectability for the characters, which reached its zenith with *Nati Binodini* (1973), a play about the nineteenth-century actress Binodini who I very briefly introduced in the previous section. Written by Brajen De, *Nati Binodini* centred on her purity of character rather than the defiant voice reflected in her autobiographical writings, and created a female star of jatra in Bina Dasgupta who played the titular role. Off stage, as 'the jatra lifestyle and projections paradoxically tend to shed all conventional standards of Bengali middle-class morality and literally challenge the domestic sphere', actresses adjusted to the male dominated hierarchy in the nomadic lifestyle by acquiescing to the patriarchal structure and thereby earning certain leeway in enjoying relationships of their own choice (Dutt 2010: 132). Actresses in jatra were essentially de-feminized professionals surviving in a ruthless co-sexual workplace (Davis 1991: 105; Dutt 2010: 132).

Contextualizing Utpal Dutt's involvement with jatra in the 1970s and 1980s within these principal historical strands facilitates better understanding of his weaving of emotional politics in the gendered dimension of nationalism, the significance of his Left politicization of jatra and his contributions in the techniques of jatra performances. In the next two sections, I shall first explore Dutt's early forays into jatra along with his writings on the form and then offer a fuller analysis of one of his most successful jatra plays, *Sannyasir Tarabari* (1972).

Utpal Dutt on and in Jatra

Dutt maintained, with typical pragmatism, that it would be erroneous to define any form as national or as something especially distinctive in terms of its locality, but rather is more useful to think in terms of what would be best liked by the largest number of people in a region or a nation (Dutt 1991: 40).

From his early days with IPTA in 1950–1951, he had suggested the leadership engage more seriously with jatra because it remained the most popular form of mass entertainment and consequently would enable them to reach a larger audience (Das 2012: 2). The tendency of jatra audiences to be boisterous, to be vocal about their likes and dislikes, Dutt felt, was a key strength of the form which evidenced its vitality (Dutt 1991: 41). Dutt identified a similarity between the jatra audience and Brecht's descriptions of the working-class audience, which would smoke and drink during the performance and remain fidgety unless the performance fully engaged its attention. The possibility of exploring this particular dimension of audience engagement presented itself when Dutt was finally invited to write for jatra companies in 1968.

Sova Sen notes in her autobiography that it was during a critical period for the Little Theatre Group in the late 1960s, that New Arya Opera – a jatra company – invited Dutt to write a play or *pala* (Sen 2017: 93). Panchu Sen, the principal actor of the jatra troupe, came to meet Dutt and an agreement was made. Dutt first went to watch New Arya Opera's performance of *Bangali* (Bengali) and was impressed by Sen's acting. As per agreement, New Arya Opera began advertising their new play *Rifle* which was to be written by Dutt. Initially Dutt decided to revise his proscenium play *Tota* (*Bullet*), which was later performed as *Maha Vidroha* (*The Great Rebellion*) (1973), based on the rebellion of 1857. However, Sen stated quite firmly that his team and the jatra space itself, was not ready for such a play. Dutt then decided to completely rewrite the play while keeping the same title. The result was also a nationalist play, but the subject matter was changed from 1857 to armed anti-colonial movement of 1930s in Bengal. When he read the new play to the troupe, Panchu Sen was overwhelmed by its potential and finally *Rifle* (1968) arrived as a new political intervention in the jatra scene. Jatra historian Prabhat Kumar Das observes that although it was not the first political play in jatra, the newness of this particular intervention came through the character of the Muslim peasant Rahamat, played by Panchu Sen, who inspired the middle-class revolutionaries to start the nationalist revolution. The play was, in jatra parlance, a 'hit' (Das 2012: 3; Sen 2017: 94).

Unfortunately, Dutt was unaware of the dubious economic practices of jatra and was ruthlessly duped by the owner of New Arya Opera, who did not pay him the promised amount even after he delivered a successful show. Dutt had almost decided to abandon jatra for good when he was approached by Shailen Mohanty first apologized on behalf of all jatra companies and then asked for another *pala*. Dutt agreed to work with him and wrote *Jallianwallahbag* (1969) (See Figure 9), a play about the mass shooting of an unarmed Indian crowd by the British military in 1919 at Jallianwallahbag in Punjab province. This time Dutt also directed. Sen recalls Dutt being pleasantly surprised by the eagerness

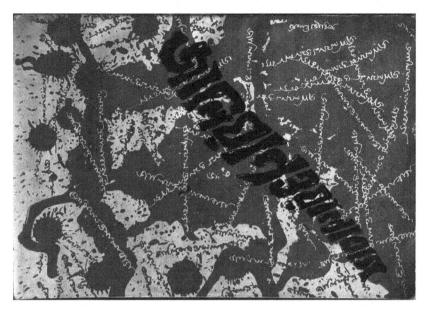

Figure 9 Published text of Jallianwallahbag, Utpal Dutt's Jatra Play

of jatra actors to learn from him, and by their dedication to embellishing their craft with the techniques he introduced in relation to synchronizing character to the rhythm of the play and unlocking the emotional depths of the scenes (2017: 99). This experience was perhaps the basis for Dutt's later claim that playwrights and actors of Bengali theatre should learn from jatra how to reach out to an audience with simplicity of plot but with great acting skill (Das 2005: 245). The success of *Jallianwallahbag* can, perhaps, be understood from a review published in popular Bengali daily *Anandabazar Patrika* (1970) which praised the jatra in rapturous ways – '*Jallianwallahbag* by Satyambar Opera deploys the emotional arc of the play so deftly yet intensely that hundreds of audiences become one in feeling excited, breathless, playful and deeply moved with the narrative'. Dutt's hope to reach out to the largest number of audiences with the form of entertainment they liked best was finally coming to fruition.

Dutt revealed in an interview with Samik Bandyopadhyay that his awareness of the fact that 'peasants and workers in the coal-mines and tea-gardens are the highest paying audiences of the Jatra' was enhanced by his experiences working in the field, and further that 'once a director or an actor comes close enough to this multitude and feels the tremendous presence of the people, he is bound to undergo a radical transformation within himself' (1972: 4). The successful political intervention he had achieved through jatra, consequently, both broadened and intensified his larger project of moving his audience towards a new political consciousness. Subsequently, the nationalist movement, which was the most recurrent theme in his plays, began to encompass different periods. Dutt wrote about the Indigo revolt of 1859 in *Neel Rakta* (The Colour of Blood is Indigo, 1970); an episode of guerrilla war by Subash Chandra Bose's Azad Hind Fauj or Indian National Army in 1944 in *Delhi Chalo* (March to Delhi, 1970); the eighteenth-century Sannyasi-Fakir rebellion against the British East India Company after the famine of 1770 in Bengal in *Sannyasir Tarabari* (The Crusade, 1972); the early years of Bengal Renaissance in nineteenth century in *Jhar* (The Storm, 1973); and an episode from the armed anti-colonial movement in Bengal in 1930s in *Baisakhi Megh* (Storm Cloud, 1974). Many of these jatras achieved popular success, and taken as a whole, they initiated a different imagining of the popular political potentials of jatra (Das 2005: 243).

In terms of narrative construction and characterization, Dutt usually relied on the established jatra conventions, creating 'fragments of intense realism and episodical intensity in these alienated conditions [the audience being fitfully attentive but also chatting, smoking and "appreciating or condemning loudly the performance itself"]' (1972: 5). His heroes were typically flawed subalterns who possessed an elevated sense of righteousness but were never dulled by an excess of virtue, while his women characters were often bold, revolutionary and iconic in their love for the nation. The specific gender politics of Dutt's jatra are interesting because of his representation of strong women, which differ from the more popular and mainstream trends of pure and chaste heroines in contemporary jatra. Discussing one of his most successful jatras, *Sannyasir Tarabari*, in more detail will give us an opportunity to understand how violence, nationalism and love were woven into and interacted in his *palas*.

Love and Political Violence in *Sannyasir Tarabari* (The Crusade, 1972)

Sannyasir Tarabari is an adaptation of Bankim Chandra Chatterjee's two novels on the Sannyasi-Fakir rebellion of 1772, *Anandamath* (1882) and *Debi Choudhurani* (1884). Tanika Sarkar's reading of these novels in her *Hindu Wife, Hindu Nation* (2003) reveals the stirrings of Hindu revivalism, a characteristic feature of late colonial Bengal, within their proto-nationalist narratives. This *pala* was Dutt's way of revisiting the complexities of geopolitical history in the consolidation of British rule in Bengal in the late eighteenth century and re-figuring the sociality of the emotions surrounding a violent peasant rebellion in terms of the decolonization of the history of peasant insurgency. In Dutt's play, Chatterjee's novels become historical allegories for the contemporary peasant unrest of the 1970s, as well as providing a critique of the masculinist political violence that pervaded Bengal in 1971.[8] Dutt responded to the combination of militarized state violence and revolutionary violence by exploring the emotional crevices of cruelty, bloodshed and perversion and by ensuring the performance of history would shine a light on the present.

Sannyasir Tarabari opens with a conversation between the Governor-General of Bengal Warren Hastings (1732–1818) and Captain Rennell (a quasi-historical figure) on the devastating effect of rapacious British tax policy in Bengal leading to the famine of 1770. It then progresses to a village where a poor Brahmin is desperate to get food for his dying daughter. The introduction of principal characters ends in the third scene where Devi Chaudhurani, a female zamindar (landowner), is introduced as an able administrator trying to keep her subjects alive in the midst of famine. Dutt creates large-scale emotional moments in the first act by unveiling exploitation by the Company, the ruthlessness of British officers and the helplessness of the rural poor. In the second act, the poor Brahmin re-emerges as another quasi-historical character, the rebel Ramananda Giri, while Devi Chaudhurani is transformed from caring mother and able administrator of her absentee husband's estate to a gun-carrying revolutionary leader who leaves her beloved child behind to join the rebellion. By allowing the tension between revolutionary commitment and domestic responsibility to escalate to tragedy – Devi's child is mercilessly tortured by the usurper landlord who conspires against Devi by falsely accusing her of adultery – Dutt fulfils the typical expectations of jatra. Subtler textures of emotion, however, emerge in the character of Rennell, who is a conflicted colonist, intensely loathing what he does to the people he is supposed to govern and yet committed to getting 'the job done'. In the third act, Ramananda Giri's, journey from compassionate revolutionary to a grotesque assassin also adds nuance. Dutt contends that in *Sannyasir Tarabari*:

> The conflicts within the revolutionaries, the delight in butchery that Ramananda Giri displays, the famine which dehumanizes the peasants, the people turning away from their own champions, the lonely revolutionaries being burnt out of their forest-hidings, the change in Rennell from an opium-smoking, tired, cultured Englishman to a savage successor of Hastings, and the revolutionary's final death in chains, totally alienated from his own people, secretly poisoned and thus deprived of even the halo of martyrdom – all these were elements built a dialectical view of the patriotic war. (Dutt 2009: 172)

---

[8] By the end of 1971, the Naxalbari movement had entered its most violent phase and the actual killings were circumscribed by the celebration of virile masculinity. The state inflicted violence on the Naxalites and their sympathisers bore an equal mark of militarized masculinity. Sinha Roy, *Gender and Radical Politics in India*, pp. 126–148

Dutt's intention in purposefully revealing revolutionary truth though a dramaturgy of contradiction is evident in this account and in the play itself.

In the dynamic space shared by love and violence, Chatterjee's novels and Dutt's play – two retellings almost a century apart – focus on the ferocity of revolutionary violence which can dehumanize revolutionaries, and the potential for love to transcend such futile violence. In the penultimate scene of the play, the stage direction reads:

> [Prison. Enter Rennell, followed by Ramananda in chains. He is encircled by British soldiers; their guns aloft]. (Dutt 1997: 447)

The scene progresses mainly through exchanges between Ramananda and Rennell on the nature of revolutionary violence and on identifying the enemy of the people of Bengal. Devi Chaudhurani enters to pay respect to Ramananda for saving her son and to convey the salute of their comrades, while Rennell retreats to the background. The romantic tension between Ramananda and Devi Chaudhurani, articulated in several earlier scenes, drives their conversation. Devi reminds him he will always be in her heart and that love for him exists among the people. Devi also urges him to strike a compromise with the Company to secure his release from the prison in order to keep the rebellion alive. Ramananda refuses even to acknowledge he once harboured romantic feelings towards Devi, and declares himself a heartless exterminator of enemies, a steel sword of the revolution. He cannot help reveal himself however:

> Rennell: I was wondering, if I were a scoundrel like Warren Hastings, I could have broken your resistance. I could have put Devi Chaudhurani in *turun*[9] and tortured her. You would have agreed to proclaim non-violence to save her.
> Ramananda: (smiling) Do you take me for such a weak person?
> Rennell: Is love a weakness? I do not think so. What I do think, is, in your entire life Devi Chaudhurani is the only ... the only ... how does one express? Brightest bloom – beauty – fruition.
> Ramananda: Devi Choudhurani is no one special in my life. I am an ascetic; I do not allow anyone to grow their roots in my existence.
> Rennell: Please refrain from such naiveté. Not to this world-weary Rennell.
> (Dutt 1997: 452)

As the excerpt confirms, despite his denial, Ramananda cannot conceal his love for Devi from Rennell, the world-weary Captain who occupies the tenuous connecting space between sophisticated English gentleman and a pitiless colonist. Rennell actually refrains from torturing Devi in front of Ramananda, revealing a glimpse of humanity within the colonial system. In addition, his reference to Warren Hastings as a 'scoundrel' confirms that he is aware of the

---

[9] *Turun* was a wooden contraption like the stocks where a person can be restrained for punishment.

brutality of the Company *Raj* and that he actively chooses not to resort to such tactics. Rennell's resistance exposes a tension within the discourses of colonialism, which finally morphs into a subtler but more heinous form of violence. At the end of the scene, Rennell poisons Ramananda, denying him the opportunity to be a martyr and thus succeeding in crushing the rebellion through deceit.

It is interesting to note the deceitful colonist insists that love is not weakness, while the emotionally exhausted revolutionary can barely conceal his desperation for an escape through martyrdom. The distinction between 'friend' and 'enemy' gets blurred at this moment as Rennell shows admiration for his enemy, even alerting him to the importance of love in retaining humanity in the face of brutal violence. It is equally interesting that Dutt uses male characters to explore doubt, suicidal thoughts and emotional vulnerability as they suffer personal crises having committed acts of revolutionary violence, or performed particularly brutal acts in order to end rebellion against the ruling authority. As the tension between love and violence transforms into a love of violence – evidenced both in Ramananda and Rennell – this nexus becomes, in Dutt's political imagination, symptomatic of the crisis of masculinity. Love for violence destroys the possibility of revolutionizing love as an equal, reciprocal, and consensual emotion. The ethical limits of love are stretched beyond peace, in the sense of absence of war, because love for violence continuously redraws the lines between compassion and ruthlessness in protecting friends and destroying enemies.

It is Devi, the female revolutionary, who emerges as the character with the clearest grasp of the meaning of resistance. She belongs to a rural landowning family and finds the courage to express her love to Ramananda Giri, when she loses her social capital and is denied her social status as a widow having been falsely accused of adultery. She becomes her own person through her fight against the British. The emotion of love, in this character, is enmeshed in romance, desire, sacrifice and finally a sense of freedom. She understands why Ramamnanda as the steel sword of revolutionary violence becomes deaf to utterances of love, and it is she who finally disappears among the people to wait for the next popular burst of revolutionary violence. Love, as Devi confirms through her words and her actions, is a much wider emotion than individual romantic love. She fights the Company and in so doing loves her people, her comrades and Ramananda with mature clarity. Her expanded sense of love looks beyond romantic love and through her Dutt thus presents another critique of patriarchy.

The huge success of this jatra, after it played 'before electrifying mass audiences for three years', confirms that this revolutionary rearticulation of love has found resonance among the people (Dutt 2009: 173). Dutt's staging of revolutionary love is achieved via clashes between, to borrow from Raymond

Williams, archaic and residual elements of male chauvinism and women's self-realization as emancipated agents, and he often makes female characters represent 'emergent' aspects of a new modern sociality (1977: 121–127). As this love is appreciated by the jatra audience, it may be possible to think about reciprocity between the playwright and the audience as a further expansion in the meaning of love. Here there is perhaps also the potential to introduce into the modern lexicon of love another Bengali term – *bhalobasa* (another indeterminate form of love like *prem*, which, however, unlike *prem* is not limited in modern Bengali to only romantic love). A successful drama of conflicted emotions, of historical conflicts between colonialism and nationalism, of conflicts between the poor and the rich, finally finds a balanced equality and reciprocity in this jatra as Dutt reinterprets *prem* and *deshprem* for his audience while the audience reciprocates by demonstrating *bhalobasa* for the play itself. The language of *prem* decolonizes itself from the its typical articulation in colonial modernity as a form of ethical romantic love, to become love for an art form, infused with a political consciousness.

4 Decolonizing Feminism: Revolutionary Women in Dutt's Plays

Women activists in India – across the spectrum of the Left and the Autonomous women's movement – were shaken when a young woman, Roop Kanwar, was immolated as a 'sati' in September 1987 in Deorala, Rajasthan. The shock, after the event, resulted in a deep introspection into the history of women's rights both academically and socially. Kumkum Sangari and Sudesh Vaid's ethnographic essay (1991), on the occurrence of sati in the Shekhawati region of Rajasthan, where the event took place in 1987, alerts us to the entangled nature of gender, class and caste within a local community that produces legitimizing narratives of sati and confirms that Roop Kanwar's immolation was not an exceptional event. Moving beyond positions of either feeling shocked by 'sati' or succumbing to innocent popular 'blind faith', Sangari and Vaid trace a grounded network of patriarchal systemic violence. They invite feminists to a more fundamental probing of consent in the context of patriarchal ideologies and beliefs which support such extreme violence against women.

Dutt, as ever sensitive to contemporary politics, responded to this event and its aftermath with *Agnishajya* (Berth of Fire) (1988). As an old guard of the committed political theatre, unceasingly engaged in revisiting the historical junctures of struggle and gleaning elements of progress, he returned to the difficult and chequered history of the reformer and thinker Ram Mohun Roy's contributions and dilemmas in attempting to prevent sati in the early decades of the nineteenth century. Among Dutt's plays *Agnishajya* stands out for its unusually pessimistic tone. In contrast to the characteristically boisterous tenor of Dutt's history plays, this pessimism exposes an unbridgeable gap between legal reform and social reality, and invites the audience, like Sangari and Vaid, to rethink how sati becomes legitimized in the social network. Dutt focuses on Raja Ram Mohun Roy's long struggle but concludes with his distancing himself from the Prevention of Sati Act of 1829. His Ram Mohun Roy says in the final scene of the play:

> Raja Radhakanta Deb [the conservative supporter of sati] and his ilk call themselves patriots, opposition to the British rule, advocates of independent India. If I were to support the law proposed by Lord Bentink, they would have equated the entire struggle against sati as part of the British colonial rule. They would have said that the British are forcibly changing Indian customs and Ram Mohun Roy has supported such impositions. They would have called us traitors to the nationalist cause. We have to stop sati with our own efforts, not with the help of the British, and definitely not with the British legal system. (Dutt 1999: 279)

This speech takes us back to Achilles Mbembe's definition of decolonization as 'an active will to community' – where the goal is 'to realize a shared project: to stand up on one's own and to create a heritage' out of the 'splendid sterility of an atrophied existence', imposed by colonialism (2021: 2–3).

The gender politics of such a process need to proceed carefully and sensitively in the way an independent democracy needs to consider its marginalized community(ies) – enabling progress without necessarily stifling the will to community. It may be useful to remember Nivedita Menon's cautionary words about the porous and contradictory borders of different orders of power of caste, race, gender and global capitalism, which shape the universal application of law, possibly changing its impact in the narratives of the said law's interpretations (2015). The *located*-ness of theories intended to challenge and change the social order – both spatially and temporally – remains crucial to understanding the performance of politics. Looking for women's agency – women's ability to react to the situations they find themselves in – in such performances of politics may be a useful strategy for understanding how political theatre, agency and decolonization become enmeshed in women's political activism.

This final section is a study of different aspects of Dutt's engagement with the 'women's question' in his theatre, from this perspective of remaining attentive to processes of decolonization. In this instance, I have focused on identifiable themes and representative characters, rather than on specific plays. My chosen themes have emerged from close-reading of the plays and from performance histories, as far as I am able to access them. The three themes I identify, and trace are solidarity, revolutionary consciousness and sacrifice. Dutt's women characters explore these themes in various complex ways whether they are larger-than-life strong characters or, more often, conflicted human beings trying to make sense of the exploitative structures within which they live.

Solidarity: Women as a Collective

I have written about solidarity amongst subaltern women in a previous section, the support for each other amongst two generations of actresses in public theatre in my discussion of *Tiner Tolowar*. The bond between Basundhara – the older actress – and Moyna, the younger heroine is expressed through Moyna's training, Basundhara's indulgent support for Moyna's relationship with Priyanath and finally in their flanking the stage while crying out in support of the nationalist cause in the nineteenth-century public theatre. In *Kallol* also the characters of Krishnabai and Lakshmibai – mother-in-law and daughter-in-law in the play – not only supportive of each other, but become comrades-in-arms during their steadfast struggle against the British Admiralty during the naval mutiny of 1946. *Kallol* begins at the end of Second World War with Shardul Singh missing for two years. Lakshmibai is compelled to remarry another sailor. At this juncture Shardul returns with his rebel ship *Khyber*. The scene, where Shardul meets Krishnabai, Lakshmibai and her second husband, remains a critical scene in the play. Krishnabai defends Lakshmibai against her own son's accusations of infidelity, saying that she has as much right to remarry as her son, especially when he was absent in their days of struggle against hunger and rapacious foreign soldiers. Krishnabai even defends Lakshmibai's second husband, saying, 'how would you know how beastly were those American marines! [. . .] who saved Lakshmi's dignity at those times? That crippled man. Once he alone defended Lakshmi against three marines, he lost his consciousness fighting them, but fell down only after Lakshmi could escape' (Sen 2017: 81). Krishnabai's support for Lakshmibai's right as a human being to choose a new partner even over her own son is an incredible feminist gesture, which is made believable because of the way Dutt builds her character through the play.

These instances of subaltern women's solidarity have led me to revisit *Teer* (Arrow) (1967). In *Teer* solidarity among subaltern women – peasant women coming from different ethnic communities – plays a significant role in ensuring the plays efficacy as successful political theatre. It preempts concerns about race and caste in forming a 'we' amongst the women characters that might lead to an almost proto-feminist solidarity. The significance of the construction of this 'we' lies in the way it figures the collective as a democratic group with internal conflicts, not as a pre-given condition through which women's issues can be organically resolved. Women's concerns are incorporated, not because of patriarchal benevolence or any urge to be inclusive, or as a compensatory gesture. Instead, female solidarity is carefully woven into the plot and made crucial to the development of revolutionary consciousness among the peasants.

Teer is based on events surrounding the peasant uprising in Prasadujote village, at the Naxalbari police station area, in May 1967 which subsequently came to be known in the annals of postcolonial India as the Naxalbari movement. On 24 and 25 May 1967 violence erupted between angry peasants and the local police in which one policeman and eleven peasants were killed, seven of whom were women. By 1967 the political debate between leaders supporting an armed movement and those supporting democratic struggle within the CPI(M) had intensified. The incident at Naxalbari ignited a long and blood-soaked conflict between the two factions after CPI(M) became part of the coalition government of West Bengal in the 1967 Assembly Elections. The news of peasants taking up arms in Prasadujote emotionally and politically influenced Dutt to such an extent that he visited the place with a couple of his comrades from Little Theatre Group. His support for the movement became evident through his play – *Teer,* which premiered in Calcutta at the Minerva on 16 December 1967. The play portrays in detail the events that led to the uprising and the horrors of police-firing on peasants. It also shows great ingenuity in depicting the reactions of the urban middle-class to the incident, but ends on a rather formulaic note, with the peasant hero successfully avenging the deaths of his fellow revolutionaries.

The status of this play in Utpal Dutt's oeuvre, has remained precarious ever since Dutt withdrew his support from the Naxalbari movement in 1970. Between 1968 and 1970, Dutt had led the life of an absconding revolutionary in order to evade arrest and was also publicly pilloried for signing a bond rescinding his right to make political theatre to ensure his release when he was finally tracked by the police (Dutt 2009: 103–105; Sen 2017: 88–91). *Teer*, meanwhile, was 'running to packed houses, until the Congress bosses and the police decided enough was enough' and, according to Dutt, sent saboteurs to break up LTG itself (2009: 101–102). 'But', by then he continues, 'the realization had finally dawned on me that my play was on the wrong side of the class struggle' and so he withdrew it (2009: 102). It is important, therefore, to pause here to clarify why I have decided to include *Teer* in a series of other plays which have more distant historical contexts. Dutt's own testimony support the play's inclusion:

> The heroism of the peasants and the wanton brutality of the police are true; it was a moment in the class struggle, a focused hour of history, an explosion of class conflict in its utter nakedness [...] When the volley of police bullets mow down the women in Prasadujot, only a 'pure' intellectual, disdaining taking sides, could remain unmoved. I was moved, and what I said in my play

is, in the final analysis, absolutely true. [. . .] it was to me, a summary of the exploits of the peasants in Telengana and Kakdwip, of the guerrilla battles of Chin-Cha-Chi district behind Japanese lines, of the courage that attempted to storm the Moncada fortress in Cuba [. . .] It has already become history [. . .]. (2009: 90–91).

Dutt locates the May Uprising of 1967 as a moment of contemporary history, then, and describes *Teer* as a document of that history, rather than as representative of the entire set of political actions that swept West Bengal – and certain other parts of India like Andhra Pradesh, Bihar and Chhattisgarh – for the next five years.

This historical background of the play is important in contextualising both its plot and its performance history. Quite early in the narrative Debari Rajbangshi succeeds in breaking the taboo of inter-community marriage and walks into the home of her beloved Jonaku (Dutt 1995: 242–245). Such a move was indeed revolutionary at that point of time in that region as oral history evidences social concern, even hostility towards inter-community love affairs (Sinha Roy 2020). This love-marriage runs into problem when Debari's literacy becomes an issue for the unlettered and superstitious Jonaku, and intense emotional interactions are created to peel away the layers of patriarchal chauvinism imbricated within the subaltern condition. The crisis is resolved when Jonaku finally realizes the value of reading to becoming a better revolutionary and turns to Debari to teach him (Dutt 1995: 264–274). Debari's revolutionary activities are supported, at various points of the play, by her women comrades, Sanjho and Gangee Oraon. Both Sanjho, with her companionate marriage to Birsa, and Gangee, with her troubled relationship with Shanicharoa, work towards revolutionary solidarity. They articulate their protests against patriarchy in the same way they register their voices against class and ethnicity-based oppression.

A curious piece of evidence shows that camaraderie among women characters on stage was repeated among the actresses playing those roles and moreover that this camaraderie became an issue of contention for the theatre group. After Dutt signed the bond, he immediately left for Bombay to shoot a film, the social atmosphere within the group became volatile. Sova Sen, his wife and an important member of LTG, writes that every member felt uneasy and combative (Sen 2017: 90). In absence of Dutt, Sen became a target for their ire. In a group meeting one member brought a list of accusations against Sen, the most serious being her intentional support for women members instead of treating everybody equally. Eventually, Sen was suspended from the group (Sen 2017: 90). Her response is worth quoting:

I was stunned to hear this. I thought that is what I should do. How would they understand what it takes to bring an actress within the group? They have never spared a thought about the issue. At least fourteen to eighteen actresses used to work in *Teer*. They came from different backgrounds, different locations with professional and amateur training. I had to take care of their requirements. Otherwise, why would they come? For what exactly? (2017: 90)

We can only be speculative about the precise motivation for such an accusation. Given the nature of the confused and confusing times, it is, perhaps, prudent to assume that for most of the metropolitan male intelligentsia who engaged with political Group Theatre, 'imagined' women characters were capable of conscious political decision precisely because they were constructions of the male imagination, while the 'real' women/actresses, with whom they had everyday interactions in the public sphere, were perceived to be 'privileged'. I am interpreting the accusations as privilege because it seems the principal grudge was against a woman in a leadership position of the group, who looked after the interests of other actresses. If we rely on the memoirs and interviews of actresses working in the professional and amateur theatre at this time we can see their situation was far from privileged (Dutta 2012). Their struggle to continue with their acting lives speak to the necessity of what Sen was implying when she spoke of 'looking after the requirements' of actresses working on *Teer*. The on and off stage solidarity of women in *Teer*, consequently, emerges as a benchmark in the history of postcolonial political theatre. They were forging a 'will to community' through a decolonization process that was far more complex than the straightforward end of foreign colonial rule.

Revolutionary Consciousness: Women Thinking Ahead

Let me continue with the example of *Teer* for this theme as well. In the seventh chapter of the play, which, like jatra is divided into chapters instead of scenes, Devidas, the urban Naxalite tries to explain the strategy of the 'people's war' by reading out from party-booklets, but his peasant comrades fail to understand the grandiloquent language. Finally Gangee Oraon stands up and speaks:

Gangee: Do you know how an Oraon hunter used to hunt elephant with a mere knife?
Somari: Hunt elephant with a knife? You are talking nonsense! A mere knife to hunt a big elephant?
Gangee: So are we! Mere arrows in front of those guns and canons!
[Everybody laughs]
Gangee: [continues] Listen carefully what happened then. The hunter thought – elephant is so big, if he would try to attack from the front the

elephant would crush him with its trunk [. . .] but he was very clever. He started to strike with knife at the hind-legs of the elephant. The elephant could not reach him because it is big and slow and the hunter was swift. Then the hunter started striking knife-wounds on both sides of the elephant's body. The elephant became tired, injured and after much blood-loss it sat down on the ground. The hunter then leapt up to its shoulder and struck the knife in its head. I think chairman Mao meant this. This state is like that elephant. The cities are its head. It has the trunk and long teeth to protect its head. So start from its hind-legs, start from far-away villages where the trunk does not reach and it takes time to turn around. So strike and duck, strike and duck. It will finally crumple down.

[Gangee sits down. Devidas looks at her with wonder and admiration.]
(Dutt 1995: 263–264)

The most remarkable aspect of this rendition of the 'parable of the elephant hunt' is that a tribal-peasant-woman has the capacity and agency to explain the conceptual strategy of guerrilla warfare (Bandyopadhyay 2000: 16–17). Her speech challenges each layer of her marginalization through ethnicity, class and gender. Dutt offers this articulation in spite of the long silence about women's revolutionary consciousness in the leadership of the Naxalbari movement. It is possible to assume that Dutt's first-hand experience of speaking to the local political activists immediately after the event of May 1967 helped him to create such women characters. The oral histories of Naxalite women, recorded nearly forty years after their participation in the movement, suggest that women took active initiative in spreading the message of their struggle (Sinha Roy 2011). 'We spoke to them about politics, about our country, our struggle' one such oral testimony explains, 'then they used to give us food, place to live and loved us for being there … [i]f we did not make them understand our politics, they then would have given us over to the police' (Sinha Roy 2011: 106–107). This confirms that women played important roles in explaining the rationale as well as the strategy of the movement

It is, perhaps, useful by way of clarification to explain that I am trying to define revolutionary consciousness in this context as something different to textbook definitions of Marxist class consciousness. I am trying to understand these women's – both real and fictional – ways of understanding the world they live in and their processes of articulating this understanding in a manner closer to Raymond Williams' description of ideology as a complicated and dynamic process within which people become conscious of their interests and their conflicts (1977: 68). In the period when Dutt was writing these plays, it was rare to think about women, especially subaltern women, as even aware of the conflicts they needed to resolve, far less as capable of explaining abstract concepts regarding that struggle or *talking politics*. Sova Sen's experience draws our attention to persistent anxiety around women's collective voice, even in the progressive environment of Leftist political theatre. If such accusations could take place in Dutt's own theatre group, it is easy to assume women's articulation of their own concerns and awareness of their potential as cultural activists remained exceptional. Against this backdrop, Dutt created strong women characters who possessed the ability to understand their own capacity as communist revolutionaries across national and historical borders. In this section, I focus on two such characters: Grandma Kim in *Ajeya Vietnam* (1966) and Frau Tsauritz in *Barricade* (1972).

In *Ajeya Vietnam*, the character of Kim – an old Vietnamese woman – emerges as an unwaveringly committed communist. Rustam Bharucha describes her as 'the voice of reason in the play' because of her critical key role in explaining the conflict in Vietnam (1983: 80). She is by turns romantic about the future of the country, quietly comforting to a wounded child, fierce in shooting down American fighter-planes, and rousing in her invective against the captured enemy. Bharucha, however, has located a seriously problematic moment where Kim asserts 'the true, faithful, chaste [Vietnamese] woman is she, who has been raped by the enemy' (Dutt 1995: 196). 'Nothing' Bharucha argues, 'can rouse the anger of a Bengali audience more than to watch a woman brutalized on stage' and yet Dutt makes 'a seventy-five-year-old character (his voice of reason in the play) urge the younger women to accept the indignity of rape' (1983: 80). For Bharucha, Grandma Kim's reasoning makes rape almost a condition for freedom and he warns 'that most feminist theatre groups in Europe and America (even those with a Marxist orientation) would not react to it favourably' (1983: 81).

Given Bharucha's status as a postcolonial theatre scholar, I would like to pay attention to this critique and explore the complexities around his claim. In all postcolonial nation-states, the process of decolonization involves specific, located ways of coming to terms with the sacrifices made in achieving independence. In public memory, women's sacrifices, especially sacrifices made in the face of political violence inflicted by the enemy, may involve a sense of shame because in case of women political violence often includes sexual violence. It is difficult for the men of postcolonial nations to come to terms with such violence because its very purpose is to emasculate, by demonstrating that these men are incapable of defending the sexual purity of *their* women. Challenging this masculinist narrative of shame, postcolonial feminists have argued the importance of considering women who have endured sexual violence as survivors and not as victims, as freedom fighters who have been tortured by the enemy. In fact, the entire narrative around rape has been challenged by postcolonial feminists to move its focus from shame to violence.

In such a context, Bharucha's's critique of Grandma Kim's statement fails to take account of its efficacy in it challenging discourses of shame surrounding rape and further, in co-opting it as a part of Vietnamese revolutionary struggle. I would like to argue that far from making rape a condition of freedom, as Bharucha suggests, Kim's statement gestures towards the feminist understanding of rape as a product of power and violence. In her analysis of *Dafa 180* (Section 180) – a feminist street play devised by Maya Rao and Anuradha Kapur in 1979 – Bishnupriya Dutt notices that it 'took on board how to codify the rape act and the embodiment of sexual violation in ways that eschewed playing the victim in conventional recognizable style' (Dutt 2022: 13). Rao and Kapur devised movements and choreography with ropes to enact the rape scene, with the woman's body in motion and not passive or purely victimized, thus portraying her as a resistant presence. In the more conventional proscenium theatre production of *Ajeya Vietnam* Grandma Kim, played by Sova Sen, calmly stood up to utter her statement. Such controlled emotion with minimalist gesture has a similar potential, nonetheless, to communicate the revolutionary consciousness of Vietnamese women to the audience, and to challenge perceptions of them as always and only victims.

The People's Little Theatre – the Little Theatre Group had been disbanded and then reorganized in the early years of 1970s – produced *Barricade* in 1972, a play based on the anti-Fascist struggle of the communists in Germany in 1933. Its plot is familiar enough. Searching for the truth behind the murder of an elderly well-respected citizen Ingebar Tsauritz, the journalist Otto Birkholtz unravels a Nazi plot against the communists. Sova Sen plays the role of Frau Tsauritz, the devoted wife and mother of their communist son Paul. She is initially devastated because all the evidence appears to indicate that the communists have killed her husband. There is a similarity here with the performance of distraught motherhood in *Kallol*, but a crucial difference lies in Frau Tsauritz's opposition, as a devout Christian, to the communists, in contrast to Krishnabai's evident revolutionary consciousness which is obvious from her very first appearance. In the course of the murder trial, Frau Tsauritz is transformed into a communist supporter, as she journeys into the world of her son's political ideology. Through her technique of intense concentration, Sen communicates a sense of solemnity in facing personal tragedy and yet also becomes radiant with a new consciousness. She travels from wounded wife and mother towards comradeship with her son – who is killed by the Nazis when Frau Tsauritz refuses to falsely testify against the communists – to revered devotion as her dead son appears in her dream as Jesus wearing the crown of thorns. Each stage of this journey is marked by different intonations in delivery, culminating in the full use of Sen's voice to quote from Bible (Luke 12:49) as she stands at the barricade with her son's comrades.

Sacrifice: Many Meanings of Martyrdom

Though both sacrifice and martyrdom have deep religious connotations, it is possible to read them as secular practices, especially the supreme act of giving one's life for revolutionary change. While exploring discourses of Christian martyrdom, Talal Asad has argued that instead searching for the symbolic significance of martyrdom as an exemplar for secular motivation, it would be more useful to look for 'its effectiveness in creating new spaces for secular action' (2003: 86). For Asad, the Christian martyrs of late antiquity were agentive not because they embraced the pain that wracked their bodies, but because 'as part of an emerging tradition, their public suffering made a difference not only to themselves (to their own potential actions) as members of a new faith but also to the world in which they lived: it required that one's own pain and the pain of others be engaged with differently' (2003: 87).

It is important to keep bear in mind, however, that the common word for martyr in Bengali is *shaheed/shahid*, a term steeped in Islamic religious convention. Asad explains that in this tradition a *shahid* is not always a wilful act because *shahada* or the process of becoming a *shahid* 'encompasses different kinds of "abnormal" death that have often not been chosen' (2009: 396). He gives examples, in a response to the critic Gil Anidjar, that include 'militants assassinated by Israeli drones, bystanders killed in Israeli air raids, and children shot by the IDF soldiers' thereby creating a clear distinction between the Christian martyr and the Islamic *shahid* in terms of the ways in which their deaths are understood by the community (2009: 396).

Unsurprisingly, in the Leftist cultural tradition of Bengal, a *shahid* is generally defined in Islamic rather than Christian terms. For example, the seven peasant women killed in the police shooting in Prasadujot in 1967 are typically referred as martyrs as well as freedom fighters in the anti-colonial movement. In Dutt's plays both martyrdom and *shahada* take place in various contexts. In this section, I have selected two acts of martyrdom, which are closer to Christian definitions and are open to secular interpretation. In *Suryashikar* (Hunting the Sun) (1971) and *Agnishajya* (1988) two women characters – Indrani and Snehamayee – are martyred for their beliefs. There are several important differences between the two deaths, and I would like to argue that these dissimilarities can be read productively through the lens of gender. My reason for selecting these examples is twofold. First, both Indrani and Snehamayee choose a painful, public death at the hands of the authorities with the intention of contributing to a larger cause. They purposefully will the community to engage with their pain and death. Second, as they have chosen this martyrdom, they signify agency, the capacity to initiate revolutionary change through ultimate sacrifice.

Suryashikar is set in ancient north India, in the period of the emperor Samudragupta. In it, Samudragupta's allegiance to Brahminical religious texts leads to a conflict between Brahminism and Buddhism, represented by the Buddhist monk Kalhan. Kalhan and his disciple Indrani make the scientific claim that the earth is round and that the moon is not a god but a planet, thus challenging the Brahminical religious belief in flat earth. Samudragupta makes every effort to force Kalhan and Indrani to recant their claims, using torture and finally deciding to kill Indrani by throwing her in front of a rogue elephant. Indrani accepts this gruesome, painful death and refuses to renounce scientific knowledge. Dutt creates a world of violence, cruelty and torture through the character of Samudragupta, his Brahmin ministers, his queen Urmila, and his military general Hayagreeb, all of whom maintain an empire by deceiving the people and denying them access to scientific truth.

The character of Indrani – described in the play as a true embodiment of beauty and brilliance – attains a kind of grace when she is tortured and finally informed about the manner of her execution. Dutt gives her a moment of humanity by allowing her to breakdown, before composing herself and preparing to face death. A slave-girl, Madhukarika, consoles Indrani by promising she will never reveal Indrani's moment of weakness, and this a chink in the amour of the larger-than-life martyr, remains a secret which only the audience witnesses. Before walking into the arena, Indrani explains her position to Hayagreeb, who has by then fallen in love with her:

> Indrani: How do I make you understand Hayagreeb? I have to die today – in front of the public. Truth will emerge victorious from my death.
> Hayagreeb: Do you have to get crushed by a rogue elephant for an illusory truth?
> Indrani: Yes. By dying smilingly in front of that bloodthirsty public I have to prove how tremendously powerful truth is. (Dutt 1997: 203)

The martyr speaks with clarity and assurance.

Dutt also creates a rupture in the metonymic chain of feminine/masculine; emotion/reason; religion/science binary, by making his martyr scientist a woman. Her final moments are gendered because they are rooted in funda-mental feminist arguments that challenge the association of the feminine with emotion and religion, and locate it beyond the logic of reason (Harding 2003). Her reasons for embracing martyrdom are based on the secular logic, following

Asad, of making the public engage with her pain and death as a means of inspiring the community to revolt against a superstitious violent empire. In addition, her beauty is also another form of subversion because it acts initially as a plot-device to compel the lecherous general Hayagreeb to fall in love, after which her brilliance and courage transform Hayagreeb into a compassionate lover who follows her into the arena to embrace the same death. Thus, the beautiful-brilliant-woman-scientist Indrani becomes a palimpsest of different kinds of challenge to the stereotyping of women.

In *Agnishajya* (See Figure 10), Dutt gives us a different interpretation of martyrdom in the figure of Snehamayee. The play opens with the death of her old landlord husband. As a young Bengali widow in early nineteenth-century Bengal, she and her two co-wives are to be made Sati for the benefit of her husband's family. Set in 1820s, *Agnishajya* offers a good amount of critical historical detail about how the Sati tradition was brought upon women by the colonial encounter. Dutt makes it clear through his staging of the figure of Ram Mohun Roy that pre-colonial Moghul rule disapproved of Sati as a ritual practice and that it could proliferate only after the East India Company received *Dewani* rights (1999: 250). A sift through the late eighteenth-century history of Company affirms that it indeed profited from disinheriting women, especially widows, through changes in legislation (Agnes 2000: 106–137; Chatterjee 2013: 149–157). Dutt pushes the feminist retelling of the history of nineteenth-century social reform further. In an intense confrontation between Radhakanta Deb, the leader of Hindu conservatism, and Ram Mohun Roy, Dutt demonstrates the extent to which women's bodies became the battleground over which progressive and conservative forces of colonial intelligentsia fought (1999: 264). The embodied emotion on stage encourages identification with the issue at stake (quite literally in *Agnishajya*) through gradual disaffection as the nuanced text reveals the unbridgeable gap between legal reform and social reality.

At first Snehamayee refuses to be a Sati and runs to Ram Mohun Roy for shelter. She displays strength of character by holding forth against the machinations of various powerful members of her husband's family and Ram Mohun's support enables her to challenge the tradition itself. However, the family members threaten that they will make Sati out of her two younger co-wives if she refuses, and she finally becomes a Sati by declaring that she is doing it willingly. Bishnupriya Dutt remembers that preparing to play the character involved intensive training in the Bengali language and a particular style of speaking signifying the world of a woman in early nineteenth-century rural Bengal (Dutt 2023). Her intellectual impulse came from reading the recently published *A Critique of Colonial India* (1985) by Sumit Sarkar and other writings emerging from Subaltern Studies. Her performance involved

অগ্নিশয্যা ১৯৮৮ - বনি রায়,পিয়ালি পাল, বিষ্ণুপ্রিয়া দত্ত

Figure 10 Agnishajya (Berth of Fire), 1988

internalizing the character and making her visible to the audience only by controlled gestures, which created a simmering energy.

Snehamayee's surrender to Sati, as an act of martyrdom, is not circumscribed by her intention to save the lives of her co-wives. The emotional-intellectual impulse of her Sati also comes from her final request to Ram Mohun Roy to start a movement for total social revolution. When Ram Mohun Roy asks her to admit in public that she had been threatened and blackmailed into submitting, she replies:

> Is that really necessary Dewanji? They know various ways of oppressing women. As long as they remain the leaders of this society, Sati will continue. You will not be able to do anything worthwhile with your movement to prevent Sati. Create a movement to transform this society Dewanji. (Dutt 1999: 266)

These words are also a call to the community to create a new society for themselves, of course. The quotation from Ram Mohun Roy's dialogue, with which I began this section is a follow-up to martyr Snehamayee's urging to the progressive intelligentsia to engage with her painful death differently.

The play ends in a sombre note as Ram Mohun Roy, realizing the futility of pursuing a legal route, refuses to sign the form of Prevention of Sati Act of 1829. He cuts a tragic figure as he prepares to leave for England amidst public humiliation. *Agnishajya* thus becomes a treatise on failure and that failure, the audience understands, is not only about the period of Ram Mohun but also about the contemporary moment of the late 1980s West Bengal. The Left Front Government was then facing serious crisis with the shadow of the failure of Soviet Socialism internationally looming and the coming of economic liberalization. The Marxist playwright in Dutt compelled him to think theoretically about despair and uncertainty, about the efficacy of political theatre in bringing revolutionary change. Snehamayee's martyrdom signals the call for a new community to emerge that could make this failure a stepping stone. Dutt could not abandon hope entirely, but a sense of foreboding envelops the final act. This can, perhaps, be also read as an inevitable part of postcolonial feminist politics that continuously struggles within itself to make its failures productive for a better future (Scott 2004).

Conclusion

Any attempt to make sense of decolonization as a process needs to take into account two aspects: both the political independence initiated by the end of colonial rule and also the intellectual project to undo the legacies of colonialism. In the last few decades, the process of decolonization, has undergone several phases. While these phases have often overlapped and continued simultaneously, rather than following one after the other, it should be acknowledged that the first phase began with a recuperative project of resurrecting non-European or precolonial forms, systems and traditions of knowledge in order to establish indigeneity as a central conceptual grid and to demonstrate the autonomy and by extension the authority of indigeneity. In case of modern Indian theatre, as mentioned in my Introduction, this phase was marked by intense engagements with the Sanskrit classical tradition and different forms of 'folk theatre'.

The phase that emerged a little later and still continues, involves identifying alternative modernities, in an attempt to demonstrate that the central conceptual system of modernity is a provincial European idea, universalized by imperialism. This phase is also shot through with an ethical dilemma regarding precolonial knowledge systems. It argues, in fact, that a total recuperation of non-colonial indigeneity is an ethical limit. As a result, the postcolonial intellectual is always already caught between a provincialized Europe and their own intellectual tradition. Though efforts to locate alternate modernities are yet to be completely exhausted, a third phase has arrived in the form of the exploration of dominant intellectual categories through interconnected histories of modern European empires. It argues that such categories of thought are not the transparent bequest of any one culture or people, but rather that such categories, when explored through interconnected histories reveal myriad histories and legacies.

Contextualizing Utpal Dutt's political theatre within these last two phases is my aim in this Conclusion. This task is made difficult but intellectually stimulating because Dutt began writing and making theatre during the phase of the creation of alternate modernities and his career as a theatre-maker was cut short by an untimely death just as he was making interesting forays into exploring interconnected histories. While plays like *Kallol* (1965), *Tiner Tolowar* (1971) and *Titu Mir* (1978) were attempts to uncover the forgotten histories of the Indian nationalist movement or to looking closely into the crevices of colonial modernity, plays on international contexts like *Ajeya Vietnam* (1966) or *Barricade* (1972) were extending solidarity towards socialist struggle across the world and making sense of the contemporary moment through an international historical lens. The latter marked his intensive engagement with the process of decolonization through co-opting the European traditions of socialist and communist thought. An interesting shift within this engagement can be seen through a play like *Neel, Sada, Lal* (Blue, White, Red 1989) where the interconnected histories of the French Revolution and Tipu Sultan's wars against the British East India Company become the principal threads of the dramatic narrative.

The recent revivals of his plays from 2018 to 2023 invite us to revisit this phase of interconnected histories from a different angle because the impetus to return to Dutt's plays adds another thread to these interconnected histories. This new thread intertwines twenty-first-century experiences of the rise of the right-wing, the global south gig-economy, and the coming of a new generation of postcolonial intellectuals. Taken together these threads compel contemporary theatre-makers to bring Dutt's work back to the stage. It is useful to mention here that the Left Front Government in West Bengal was defeated in the 2011 Legislative Assembly election by a centrist political party Trinamool Congress and has consistently lost popular support since this electoral setback. In the cultural scenario of the province, however, and especially in the tradition of Group Theatre, the Left has managed to continue its existence, though less as political party than as a broad ideological orientation.

Let me first list some of these revivals, with the caveat that this list is not exhaustive. I have already mentioned the revival of *Titu Mir*. Along with *Titu Mir* came *Ghum Nei* (1959), a play on the significance of the workers' union, which is now regularly performed by the theatre group Iccheymoto to warm receptions and has received awards for its sets, sound and performance. Sourav Palodhi, the director of the 2018 revival, has argued that this play has contemporary resonance because it underlines the importance of the workers' collective voice in sustaining the secular ethos of Indian democracy (Palodhi 2023). Similarly, *Barricade* (1972), which comments on the rise of authoritarianism against the backdrop of the rise of Nazism in Germany, was revived by the theatre group Chakdaha Natyajan in January 2022 to comment on the contemporary crises of religious fundamentalism and political violence in India. Another Dutt play *Ekla Chalo Re* (1989) which re-tells the history of Partition and the subsequent religious riots through the historical moment of Gandhi's assassination in 1948, was successfully revived by the group Swapna Sandhani in 2019. In September 2022, Ashoknagar Natya Anan, a Kolkata-based theatre group, staged Dutt's *Delhi Chalo* (1970), which revolves around a secret guerrilla mission of the Indian National Army, led by Subhash Chandra Bose, in 1944. The director Chandan Sen and actors in the *Delhi Chalo* company have said in an interview with *Siti Cinema* (Sen 2022) ('Utpal Dutter Kaljoyee Natok Delhi Chalo') that they produced the play to commemorate the seventy-fifth year of India's national independence, but they specifically chose a Dutt play because they wanted to mark the occasion outside the statist right-wing narration of the history of India's independence struggle. Suman Mukhopadhyay, the director of the revival of Dutt's *Ajker Shahjahan* (1985), which premiered on 15 April 2023, says that in spite of the absence of any direct political reference, the play critically reflects on the generational divides or the tenuous bridges between generations of passionate artists, making it a political play in terms of clashes between artistic ideologies Suman Mukhopadhyay, taken in September 2023.

In the remainder of this Conclusion, I will focus on three revivals – *Titu Mir, Ghum Nei* and *Ajker Shahjahan* – in order to explore how the processes of decolonization are interwoven into interconnected histories of modern European empires, challenging their legacies through the formation of new artistic languages. This is perhaps, I suggest, the most productive way to think through Utpal Dutt's legacy as a political artist. It is important to note that these three plays use Dutt's dramaturgy very differently. The revivals have effectively adapted, interpolated, even added nuances of contemporary conditions, while keeping the foundational spirit of Dutt's politics in challenging authoritarianism and values of freedom intact.

The 2019 revival of *Titu Mir* follows Dutt's text completely without altering a single sentence of dialogue but brings a different energy to it with a particular kind of physical acting and scenography that keeps the entire production mobile. Joyraj Bhattacharjee, the director, has said that Dutt's text challenged him to make the context of political struggle described accessible to his audience and that is the reason for making his actors exude energy by continuously walking through uneven rostra, leaping over scattered stage props and climbing up and down the huge bamboo structure that constitutes the principal set (Bhattacharjee 2022). This mobility literalizes the production's effort to reanimate memories of Muslim freedom fighters against colonialism, an aspect of history and collective memory that the current

Indian government is determined to erase. *Titu Mir* in 2019 or in 2023 thus becomes an act of challenging the Hindutva ideology, the right-wing political force in India that propagates Islamophobia. The revival attains new meaning within the process of decolonization as the audience gets re-oriented with regard to the multi-ethnic, multi-religious, multi-lingual history of India, and specifically to the way in which Muslims played their part in the movement towards national independence.

Ghum Nei (Without Sleep), which was revived in 2018, was written as a short one-act play about a group of long-distance truck drivers, who get stuck in a road-side halt because of a faulty bridge over the nearby river. The precarity of their situation becomes its principal theme. Sourav Palodhi, who directed the revival, has argued that he was struck by similarities between the truck drivers of Dutt's play and the gig economy workers of contemporary India. The same precarity of labour is repeating itself in the material conditions of workers in food and groceries delivery, private hire transportation, cleaning and domestic work. Palodhi reports that a member of his group read out *Ghum Nei* in one of their regular meetings because he found an uncanny resonance with Dutt's characters in his own life as a gig economy worker (Palodhi 2023). Perhaps because the contemporary relevance of Dutt's play remains so strong, Palodhi kept the original did not feel the need to contemporize it or alter its focus on truck drivers, instead adding extra dialogue developed through research on similar experiences among contemporary truck drivers near Calcutta and changing the name of the principal heroic character from the Hindu Bhabani to the Muslim Akhlaq. This change of name was a clear statement of resistance to Hindutva ideology. The scenography of the revival was realistic, even historical in that it recreated a road-side halt from 1960s, and Palodhi added a sequence of the collective chanting of *ghum nei* by the assembled truck drivers while entering and occupying the stage, two of them hold aloft a hammer and a sickle as the lights turned red. This very direct reference to Marxist political struggle also incorporates the play into the conception of decolonization as a project oriented towards the future. By refusing to consider the fall of European socialism as the final moment of failure, but rather utilizing it in a renewed effort to think about the postcolonial future.

The 2023 revival of *Ajker Shahjahan* (Shahjahan of Today) Dutt's play about the confrontation between a reclusive old theatre actor and a young film director who wants the actor to play a role of a clown in his new film, seems less obviously political in its contemporary resonances. In this narrative, the old actor first resists but finally decides to do the film because he is persuaded by the passion of the young director. The drama focuses on the tension between realistic film acting, demanded by the director, and the older actor's capacity to cope with the

Figure 11 Utpal Dutt. From Family Album

challenges this presents. The play's politics are thus understated, but it becomes an emotional minefield when the director takes his demand for realism too far by forcing the actor to roll down a steep hillside. The ensuing accident results in the old actor losing his memory, and it is precisely this memory that has sustained him for years in terms of both memorizing and memorializing his theatre roles. The revival's production design utilizes the visual strategy of projecting close-ups of the actor performing the role alongside the actions on stage, creating a continuous interaction between artistic languages. Other than incorporating a few contemporary references the director largely remains faithful to Dutt's original text but the dramaturgy and staging make clear if subtle political statements about significance of memory in building understandings of the contemporary, and consequently in shaping the future.

Finally, Utpal Dutt's legacy in Indian theatre remains dependent on and is shaped by these new interpretations of his theatre. His work created a reservoir of memory and his approach to theatre-making provides a constant reminder of the importance of history in fashioning the present. The future, however, is being shaped here and now by a new generation of directors, actors and dramaturgs who are making Dutt relevant again, and interpreting his work in ways that facilitate better understanding of the conceptual and material spaces the new postcolonial generation occupies. The process of decolonization in the political theatre of Utpal Dutt thus remains a vital part of an ongoing movement where every act of thinking and performing is revising, recreating, reinterpreting history (See Figure 11). Instead of romanticizing the past, this movement is taking shape as a critical multidimensional re-looking at the past, as a working method for making sense of collective political and artistic struggles.

Bibliography

Primary Source:

Dutt, U. (1995) *Utpal Dutt Natak Samgra: Tritiya Khanda* [Utpal Dutt Collected Plays: 3rd Volume], Calcutta: Mitra and Ghosh

Dutt, U. (1997) *Utpal Dutt Natak Samgra: Pancham Khanda* [Utpal Dutt Collected Plays: 5th Volume], Calcutta: Mitra and Ghosh

Dutt, U. (1998) *Utpal Dutt Natak Samgra: Shashtha Khanda* [Utpal Dutt Collected Plays: 6th Volume], Calcutta: Mitra and Ghosh

Dutt, U. (1999) *Utpal Dutt Natak Samgra: Saptam Khanda* [Utpal Dutt Collected Plays: 7th Volume], Calcutta: Mitra and Ghosh

Dutt, U. (2011) *Utpal Dutt Natak Samgra: Nabam Khanda* [Utpal Dutt Collected Plays: 9th Volume], Calcutta: Mitra and Ghosh

Dutt, U. (1998) *Utpal Dutt Gadya Sangraha: Pratham Khanda* [Utpal Dutt Collected Writings: 1st Volume], Calcutta: Mitra and Ghosh

Dutt, U. (2009) *Towards a Revolutionary Theatre*, Calcutta: Seagull

Garo Hill Cine-Theatre, 'In Conversation with Utpal Dutt: Interview by Surojit Ghosh', available at, https://www.youtube.com/watch?v=bgBPhsf-otg (accessed 21st September, 2023)

Hatch, James, V. (1968) 'The Communist Theatre and Utpal Dutt', *Natya Shodh Sansthan* (Archives at Natya Shodh, Calcutta), File no. CF/187

Interview with Bishnupriya Dutt, August, 2023

Interview with Joyraj Bhattacharya, August 2022

Interview with Sourav Palodhi, September, 2023

Interview with Suman Mukhopadhyay, September 2023

Mirchi Agni, *facebook live with Ajker Shahjahan* on 13th April, 2023, available at, https://www.facebook.com/watch/live/?ref=watch_permalink&v=62220 92174503157 (accessed on 24th September, 2023)

Sahapedia, 'On Utpal Dutt and His Theatre: In Conversation with Samik Bandyopadhyay', available at, https://www.youtube.com/watch?v= LlvdX1KrXSk (accessed 21st September, 2023)

Siti Cinema, 'Utpal Dutter Kaljoyee Natok Delhi Chalo', available at https://www.youtube.com/watch?v=uzduizHRAOU&fbclid=IwAR0RObmok XDz2jTjJdCJFMR7NYcA1ge07AVDbkdQLyW1mmSmtEaofdELcWY (accessed on 21st September, 2023)

Titu Mir, *facebook post*, available at, https://www.facebook.com/Titumir.col lective/posts/160238771980605, (accessed 21st September, 2023).

Secondary Sources:

Agnes, F. (2000). 'Women, Marriage and the Subordination of Rights' in Chatterjee, P. and P. Jeganathan, (eds). *Subaltern Studies XI: Community, Gender and Violence*, New York: Columbia University Press, pp. 106–137

Asad, T. (2003). *Formations of the Secular: Christianity, Islam, Modernity*, Stanford: Stanford University Press.

Asad, T. (2009). 'Response to Gil Anidjar', *Interventions*, 11(3), pp. 394–399

Bandyopadhyay, S. and U. Dutt (1972) 'Utpal Dutt Interviewed', *Enact*, 68–69, pp. 1–6

Bandyopadhyay, R. (2000). *Journal Sottor* [Journal '70s]. Calcutta: Mitra and Ghosh Publishers.

Bharucha, R. (1983). *Rehearsals of Revolution: The Political Theatre of Bengal*, Honolulu: University of Hawaii Press

Bharucha, R. 1993. *Theatre and the World: Performance and Politics of Culture*, London and New York: Routledge.

Bhatia, N. (1999). 'Staging the 1857 Mutiny as "The Great Rebellion": Colonial History and Post-Colonial Interventions in Utpal Dutt's "Mahavidroh"'. *Theatre Journal*, 51(2), pp. 167–184

Bhatia, N. (2004). *Acts of Authority, Acts of Resistance: Theatre and Politics in Colonial and Postcolonial India*, Ann Arbor: University of Michigan Press

Bhattacharya, B. (2024, forthcoming). *Colonialism, World Literature and the Making of the Modern Culture of Letters*, Cambridge: Cambridge University Press

Bhattacharya, M. (1983). 'The IPTA in Bengal.' *Journal of Arts and Ideas*, 2 (January–March), pp. 5–22.

Chakrabarty, D. (2002). *Provincializing Europe: Postcolonial Thought and Historical Difference*, New Delhi: Oxford University Press.

Chatterjee, I. (2013). *Forgotten Friends: Monks, Marriages, and Memories of Northeast India*, Delhi: Oxford University Press

Chatterjee, P. (1997). *Our Modernity*, Rotterdam: SEPHIS CODESRIA

Chatterjee, P. (2016). 'Theatre and the Publics of Democracy: Between Melodrama and Rational Realism', *Theatre Research International*, 41(3), pp. 202–217

Chatterjee, S. (2007). *The Colonial Staged: Theatre in Colonial Calcutta*, Calcutta: Seagull Books

Chattopadhyay, S. (1998). 'Natok Porichiti' [Reference for the Plays] in *Utpal Dutt Natak Samgra: Shashtha Khanda*, Calcutta: Mitra and Ghosh, pp. 653–661.

Chaudhuri, R. (2009). 'Michael Madhusudan Datta and the Marxist Understanding of the Real Renaissance in Bengal', *Economic and Political Weekly*, 44(45), pp. 61–70

Chowdhury, P. (2023). 'The Sword Unsheathed: Utpal Dutt's *Tiner Tolowar* and Crisis of Performance: A Postmodern Reading' in Gooptu, S. and M. Pandit (eds) *Performance and Culture of Nationalism: Tracing Rhizomatic Lived Experiences of South, Central and Southeast Asia*, London: Routledge, pp. 181–192.

Das, P. (2005) 'Utpal Dutt: TaNr Jatra' [Utpal Dutt: His Jatra] in Saha, N. (ed) *Utpal Dutt: Ek Samagrik Abolokan*, Calcutta: Utpal Dutt Natyotsab 2005 Committee, pp. 241–249

Das, P. (2012) 'Utpal Dutter Jatra' [Jatra of Utpal Dutt], *Naba Patrika*, 11th November, pp. 1–4

Dasgupta, A. (1983). 'Titu Meer's Rebellion: A Profile', *Social Scientist*, 11 (10), pp. 39–48

Davis, T. (1991). *Actress as Working Women: Their Social Identity in Victorian Culture*, London: Routledge

Deb Barman, D. (2014). 'When the Popular is Political: The Case of Utpal Dutt's Jatra, with Focus on "Sanyasir Tarobari"', *Indian Literature*, 58(6), pp. 183–191

Dharwadker, A. B. (2005). *Theatres of Independence: Drama, Theory and Urban Performance in India since 1947*, Iowa: University of Iowa Press

Dutt, B. and U. Sarkar Munsi. (2010). *Engendering Performance: Indian Women Performers in Search of An Identity*, New Delhi: Sage

Dutt, B. (2022). *Maya Rao and Indian Feminist Theatre*, Cambridge: Cambridge University Press.

Dutta, K. (2012). *Nijer Kothay, Tukro Lekhay*, in S. Bandyopadhyay (ed) *Ketaki Dutta: Nijer Kothay, Tukro Lekhay*, Calcutta: Thema Books

Dutt, U. (2005) 'Little Theatre O Ami' [Little Theatre and I], in Saha, N. (ed) *Utpal Dutt: Ek Samagrik Abolokan*, Calcutta: Utpal Dutt Natyotsab 2005 Committee, pp. 439–463

Dutt, U. (1994) 'Amar Natoke Sangeet' [Music in My Theatre], *Jugantar*, 27th March, pp-6–7

Dutt, U. (2014), 'Dinabandhu Mitra – Mohamuktir Khatiyan' [A critical Review of Dinabandhu Mitra], in Mukhopadhyay, A. (ed) *Epic Theatre Subarna Jayanti Sankalan: Pratham Khanda*, Calcutta: Deep Prakashan, pp. 203–273

Forsyth, A. and C. Gregson. (2009). *Get Real: Documentary Theatre Past and Present*, London: Palgrave Macmillan

Fisher, T. (2023). *The Aesthetic Exception: Essays on Art, Theatre and Politics*, Manchester: Manchester University Press.

Ghosh, G. P. (1996). *Jatra Shilper Itihas*, [History of Jatra Culture], Calcutta: Pushpa Prakashan

Ghosh, S. and U. Dutt (1991) 'Je Natoker Rajneeti Bhul, Tar Sob Bhul' [Wrong politics in a play makes it all wrong], *Desh*, 30th March, pp. 33–45.

Guha, R. (ed) (1982). *Subaltern Studies: Writings on South Asian History and Society*, Delhi: Oxford University Press

Gunawardana, A. J. and U. Dutt (1971) 'Theatre as a Weapon. An Interview with Utpal Dutt', *The Drama Review*, (15) 2, pp. 224–237

Halliday, F. (1969) 'Students of the World Unite' in Cockburn, A and Blackburn, R (eds) *Student Power: Problems, Diagnosis, Action*, Harmondsworth: Penguin Books, pp. 287–326

Harding, S. (2003). 'Why Has the Sex/Gender System Become Visible Only Now?' in S. Harding and M. B. Hintikka (eds) *Discovering Reality: Feminist Perspectives on Epistemology, Metaphysics, Methodology, and Philosophy of Science*, Dordrecht: D. Reidel Publishing Company, pp. 311–324

Issacharoff, M. (1989). *Discourse as Performance*, Stanford: Stanford University Press

Jameson, F. (1984) 'Periodizing the 60s', *Social Text*, No. 9/10, pp. 178–209

Kaviraj, S. (1995). *The Unhappy Consciousness: Bankimchandra Chattopadhyay and the Formation of Nationalist Discourse in India*. Delhi: Oxford University Press.

Kaviraj, S. (2014). *The Invention of Private Life: Literature, Identity*, New York: Columbia University Press.

Marx, K. (1947) *Notes on Indian History (664–1858)*, Moscow: Foreign Language Press

Mbembe, A. (2021). *Out of the dark Night: Essays in Decolonization*, New York: Columbia University Press.

McAuley, G. (1999). *Space in Performance: Making Meaning in Theatre*, Ann Arbor: University of Michigan Press

Menon, N. (2015). 'Is Feminism about 'Women'? A Critical View on Intersectionality from India', *Economic and Political Weekly*, 50(17), pp. 37–44.

Mancha Rasik (1966) "Minervay 'Ajeya Vietnam'" [*Ajeya Vietnam* in Minerva]. *Darpan*, 25th November

Mitra, S. and U. Dutt (2014) 'Rajnaitik Netritwa Dayitwa Palan Kare Ni: Utpal Dutt' [The political leadership did not take up the responsibility: Utpal Dutt], in Mukhopadhyay, A. (ed) *Epic Theatre Subarna Jayanti Sankalan: Pratham Khanda*, Calcutta: Deep Prakashan, pp. 62–72

Okhlopkov, N. (1966), 'From the Producer's Exposition of *Hamlet*' in *Shakespeare in the Soviet Union: A Collection of Articles*, Moscow: Progress Publishers, pp. 182–203

Pandit, M. (2015). 'Balancing Act: Swadeshi "Jatra" Performance and Engendering a Nuanced National Identity', *Social Scientist*, 43(7/8), pp. 25–39

Patnaik, P. et al (2017). *The Progressive Cultural Movement: A Critical History*, Delhi: SAHMAT

Pradhan, S. (1979). *Marxist Cultural Movement in India: Volume 1*, Calcutta: National Book Agency

Redmond, J. (ed)(1987). *The Theatrical Space*, Cambridge: Cambridge University Press

Reinelt, J. and J. Roach. (eds)(1992). *Critical Theory and Performance*, Ann Arbor: University of Michigan Press

Roy, A. (2014). *Cultural Communism in Bengal*, Delhi: Primus Books.

Roy, S. (2012[1966]), *Bharate Krishak Bidroha O Ganatantrik Sangram*, [Peasant Insurgency and Democratic Struggle in India] Kolkata: Radical Impression

Samuel, R. (ed) (1981). *People's History and Socialist Theory*, London: Routledge

Sangari, K. and S. Vaid. (1991). 'Institutions, Beliefs, Ideologies: Widow Immolation in Contemporary Rajasthan', *Economic and Political Weekly*, 26(17): WS2-WS18.

Sarkar, P. (1975). 'Jatra: The Popular Traditional Theatre in Bengal, *Journal of South Asian Literature*, 10(2/4), pp. 87–107.

Sarkar, S. (1983). *A Critique of Colonial India*, Calcutta: Papyrus

Sarkar, T. (2003). *Hindu Wife, Hindu Nation: Community, Religion, and Cultural Nationalism*, Delhi: Permanent Black.

Scott, J. W. (2004). 'Feminism's History' in Morgan, S. (ed) *The Feminist History Reader*, London: Routledge, pp. 387–398.

Sen, S. (2017). *Smarane Bismarane: Nabanna Theke Laldurga*, [Memories and Forgetting: From *Nabanna* to *Lal* Durga], Calcutta: M. C. Sarkar

Singh, L. (2011). 'Transgression of Boundaries: Women of IPTA', *Social Scientist* 39(11/12), pp. 63–72.

Sinha Roy, M. (2011). *Gender and Radical Politics in India: Magic Moments of Naxalbari (1967–1975)*, London: Routledge

Sinha Roy, M. (2020). 'The Romantic Manifesto: Gender and "Outlaw" Emotions in the Naxalbari Movement' in Arunima, G. et al (eds) *Love and Revolution in the Twentieth-Century Colonial and Postcolonial World: Perspectives from South Asia and Southern Africa*, London: Palgrave Macmillan, pp. 203–229.

Solga, K. (2019). *Theory for Theatre Studies: Space*, London: Bloomsbury

Stephens, J. (2013), 'The Phantom Wahhabi: Liberalism and the Muslim Fanatic in mid-Victorian India', *Modern Asian Studies*, 47(1), pp. 22–52.

'Su Avinito Rifle' [Well Acted *Rifle*] *Anandabazar Patrika*, 27th Feb, 1970.

Watson, J. K. and G. Wilder. (2018). (eds.) *The Postcolonial Contemporary: Political Imaginaries of the Global Present*, New York: Fordham University Press

Williams, R. (1977). *Marxism and Literature*, Oxford: Oxford University Press

Acknowledgements

The first ideas of this Element grew out of my association with theatre and performance studies scholars in Jawaharlal Nehru University and Warwick University over several years and the collaborative project 'Cultures of the Left', funded by the British Academy. My interest in political theatre practitioners in Bengal developed through several stages of learning to critically appreciate their efforts and their theatre productions. The final result of these academic and cultural engagements is the writing of this Element and it owes immensely to many people, most of all to Bishnupriya Dutt who literally opened the doors to her family home and encouraged me to conceptualize this project on her father Utpal Dutt. She has contributed generously through comments and suggestions. Silvija Jestrovic and Ameet Parameswaran read different drafts and helped with suggestions. I would like to take this opportunity to thank them for their kindness. My heartfelt thanks to Indu Jain, Komita Dhanda, Trina Nileena Banerjee, Milija Gluhovic, Urmimala Sarkar Munsi, Sayandeb Chowdhury and all members of International Federation of Theatre Research's Feminist Theatre Working Group, for listening to my ideas, reading my drafts and giving me the confidence to write about political theatre. My special thanks to Trish Reid, the best editor I could ever have to prepare the manuscript, and Samik Bandyopadhyay for sharing his vast experience of theatre in Bengal. I thank Suman Mukhopadhyay, Joyraj Bhattacharjee and Sourav Palodhi for sharing their experiences of recreating Utpal Dutt's plays in the contemporary times. I thank the librarians and staff at the archives of Natya Shodh Sansthan in Kolkata and Jawaharlal Nehru University Library. Ahvana Paul helped me to select the images from the family archive of Utpal Dutt and I cherish the days spent happily together browsing through old photo albums. I would also like to thank all members of People's Little Theatre for making me a part of their group.

My family has always been supportive of my work. My father, Prabir Sinha Roy took me to watch plays from my childhood and his enthusiasm for theatre has inspired me to start working on political theatre. Finally, thanks to Baidik Bhattacharya for sharing my journey.

Cambridge Elements ≡

Theatre, Performance and the Political

Trish Reid

University of Reading

Trish Reid is Professor of Theatre and Performance and Head of the School of Arts and Communication Design at the University of Reading. She is the author of *The Theatre of Anthony Neilson* (2017), *Theatre & Scotland* (2013), *Theatre and Performance in Contemporary Scotland* (2024) and co-editor of the *Routledge Companion to Twentieth-Century British Theatre* (2024).

Liz Tomlin

University of Glasgow

Liz Tomlin is Professor of Theatre and Performance at the University of Glasgow. Monographs include *Acts and Apparitions: Discourses on the Real in Performance Practice and Theory* (2013) and *Political Dramaturgies and Theatre Spectatorship: Provocations for Change* (2019). She edited *British Theatre Companies 1995–2014* (2015) and was the writer and co-director with Point Blank Theatre from 1999–2009.

Advisory Board

About the Series

Elements in Theatre, Performance and the Political showcases ground-breaking research that responds urgently and critically to the defining political concerns, and approaches, of our time. International in scope, the series engages with diverse performance histories and intellectual traditions, contesting established histories and providing new critical perspectives.

Cambridge Elements ≡

Theatre, Performance and the Political

Printed in the United States
by Baker & Taylor Publisher Services